Basketball

Basketball

JERRY KRAUSE, Ed.D.

Director of Instruction
Department of Physical Education
United States Military Academy
West Point, NY

Research Chair, National Association of Basketball Coaches

Series Editor
SCOTT O. ROBERTS, Ph.D.

Department of Health, Physical Education, and Recreation
Texas Tech University
Lubbock, TX

Boston Burr Ridge, IL Dubuque, IA Madison, WI
New York San Francisco St. Louis
Bangkok Bogotá Caracas Lisbon London Madrid Mexico City
Milan New Delhi Seoul Singapore Sydney Taipei Toronto

WCB/McGraw-Hill

A Division of The McGraw-Hill Companies

WINNING EDGE SERIES: BASKETBALL

This book is printed on acid-free paper.

1 2 3 4 5 6 7 8 9 0 DOC/DOC 9 3 2 1 0 9 8

ISBN 0–8151–5184–5

Vice president and editorial director: *Kevin T. Kane*
Publisher: *Edward E. Bartell*
Executive editor: *Vicki Malinee*
Editorial coordinator: *Tricia R. Musel*
Senior marketing manager: *Pamela S. Cooper*
Editing associate: *Joyce Watters*
Production supervisor: *Deborah Donner*
Coordinator of freelance design: *Michelle D. Whitaker*
Senior photo research coordinator: *Lori Hancock*
Senior supplement coordinator: *David A. Welsh*
Compositor: *Shepard Poorman Communications Corp.*
Typeface: *10/12 Palatino*
Printer: *R.R Donnelley & Sons Company/Crawfordsville, IN*

Cover image: © *Bill Leslie Photography*

Library of Congress Cataloging-in-Publication Data

Krause, Jerry, 1936– .
  Basketball / Jerry Krause. — 1st ed.
    p. cm.
  Includes bibliographical references (p.   ) and index.
  ISBN 0–8151–5184–5
  1. Basketball. I. Title. II. Series: Winning edge series
(Boston, Mass.)
GV885.K67 1999
796.323—dc21   98–37664
                                         CIP

PREFACE

Basketball is designed as a game of finesse and reason. It is an American team game that many love as a perfect blend of individualism and group effort. Playing the game for recreation and competition is enhanced by knowing the game—its history, equipment and facilities, and the rules that govern the sport.

Young and Old participate in basketball, one of the greatest American sports. The game is played indoors and on playgrounds. People with various skill levels play, from the physically challenged to professional athletes. As a major recreational sport, people play competitively or for fun. Lace up your basketball shoes, put on a T-shirt and shorts, and come join us as we look at the first American-made team sport.

▶ Audience

This text is designed for anyone who plays or watches basketball, as well as for students in basketball activity courses at the college or high school level. It can also be used as a basic, user-friendly tool to help you develop your game.

▶ Features

Basketball contains the basketball basics as well as perspectives of the game and team play essentials. As an introduction, this text explains the history, facilities, equipment, and rules of the game. While the first couple of chapters examine these areas, the rest of the book moves on to detail the preparation of the game. Individual chapters describe dynamics of the basic skills such as rebounding, ballhandling, shooting, and individual moves for "inside" and "outside" player positions. Specifically, chapters 4 through 9 focus on the critical individual fundamental skills of basketball and these are developed in a sequential, progressive manner. All other chapters center on team play, continued skill development by position (perimeter play, post play), and the important topic of conditioning for basketball.

In addition, this text offers special features that enhance its use:

- Each chapter has a bulleted list of objectives and a closing summary to reiterate the major points.
- Key terms are highlighted in boldface type and definitions are provided. This feature enables you to build a working vocabulary of concepts and principles necessary for beginning, developing, and maintaining your game.
- "Performance Tip" boxes outline techniques, applications, and strategies for quick reference.

- Assessments appear at the end of the applicable chapters to assist you in practicing your skills and improving game performance.
- The appendices offer a glossary, skill checklists, and self-evaluation checklists.
- A suggested reading list is included at the end of the book.

▶ Ancillaries

To facilitate use of this text in the classroom, a printed Test Bank is available to instructors. These multiple choice and essay questions allow for quick assessment of the basic rules and principles of basketball.

▶ Acknowledgements

This book is dedicated to my loving sister, Chrystal, my lifelong friend and supporter. She has always been an inspiration to me.

Thanks to the reviewers at Liberty University, the University of Florida, and the University of Texas—Pan American, who provided excellent feedback and to my new developmental editor, Tricia Musel, for her guidance.

CONTENTS

Contents

THE GAME—
A LOOK AT THE HISTORY

OBJECTIVES

After reading this chapter, you should be able to:

* Identify the origin of the game.
* Identify historic milestones of basketball.
* Give a basic history of the game of basketball.
* Characterize the game today.

KEY TERMS

While reading this chapter, you will become familiar with the following terms:

▶ **Basketball**

▶ **James Naismith**

▶ **National Collegiate Athletic Association (NCAA)**

A Historical Fact

Basketball is an American team "keepaway" game developed by a Canadian, James Naismith, in 1892 at Springfield College (MA). It is played and watched around the world.

ORIGIN OF BASKETBALL

Basketball is the first major team sport invented in the United States. This "new sport on the block" has only existed since 1892 and celebrated its hundredth anniversary in 1992 with special events held around the world.

Basketball came about because of the need for an indoor recreational sport during the long winters when the outdoor sports could not be played.

Springfield College in Massachusetts was the location of the national training school for the Young Men's Christian Association (YMCA). Luther Halsey Gulick, director of the physical education department, gave a young graduate student instructor, **James Naismith,** the responsibility for creating an indoor game (Figure 1-1). He was asked to solve the sticky problem of coming up with a completely new recreational activity that would interest the YMCA students and keep them busy and out of trouble during the tough New England winters.

Naismith was a native Canadian who had been exposed to soccer, football, duck on a rock (a game in which a ball was tossed at a goal), and lacrosse. He combined the elements of these games with the creative goal of throwing a soccer ball through an elevated basket—thus *basketball* (Figure 1-2). Two peach baskets (with bottoms) were nailed to the balcony on each end of the gymnasium at a height of ten feet and basketball was born. Basketball, originally intended only for indoor recreation, has also become a competitive team game that is played indoors and outdoors. Over 40 percent of games worldwide are played outdoors. The purpose of this team game is to put the ball in your basket while keeping the other team from putting the ball in their basket. Naismith's ideas resulted in a team "keepaway" game that attained world wide popularity.

Today basketball is played everywhere, but mostly indoors on a rectangular court with elevated baskets

FIGURE 1-1 Dr. Naismith.

(ten feet high) mounted on vertical backboards. The baskets are metal rings on a horizontal target for a player to throw (shoot) the ball in the air so that it goes into the basket for a score.

SPREAD OF THE GAME

The new game was a huge and immediate success with the YMCA students. Within a short time, basketball was being played across the United States and in Naismith's native Canada. The game spread rapidly as the YMCA students graduated and took the game with them all over the country and to other countries in their new positions as YMCA directors. Basketball's rise in popularity also resulted from its adaptability—an indoor sport (recreational plus competitive) for all skill levels and genders.

FIGURE 1-2 Action picture of the game.

SIGNIFICANT MILESTONES

The game spread like wildfire. There were several significant milestones in the development and growth of basketball. These milestones were the development of standardized rules, the coaching profession, international basketball, and tournaments.

THE RULES

The basketball rules were, initially, a list of thirteen typewritten statements that James Naismith posted on the gymnasium bulletin board in December of 1891 (chapter 3). The rules were first published in the college newspaper in January

▶ **Basketball**

The United States' first major team sport; invented around 1892.

▶ **James Naismith**

The inventor of basketball, a game originally intended for only indoor recreation.

1892 and later that year printed in book form. The first basketball Rules Committee was formed in 1895 and eventually led to several groups of rules committees as seen today. High schools, colleges, professionals, and international basketball all have separate rules. These rules and their development have served well to standardize and provide the operating boundaries for playing the game. Basketball officials, called referees and umpires, enforce the rules of the game.

THE COACH

The first coach was Forrest "Phog" Allen, a student of Naismith at Kansas University (where Naismith was director of athletics). Baker University (Kansas) hired Phog Allen as a basketball coach in 1907. When Allen was hired to coach, Naismith stated, "Basketball is meant to be played and not coached." Allen was hired at Kansas University in 1910 and coached there for forty-six years. The University of Kansas plays in the Phog Allen Field House. The acceptance of basketball coaching as a profession fostered the continued development of the game and improvements in the level of competition.

Coaching proved to be a difficult challenge. The game is simple yet challenging, because it is a continuous game where all players can play anywhere on the court and must play both offense and defense. The challenge is to keep the game simple to play in honor of its origins. This means that each player needs to be aware of developing into a successful basketball player with the necessary skills, the ability to play with a team; and, even more importantly, enjoys the game of basketball.

AN OLYMPIC SPORT

Basketball was played for the first time as an Olympic sport in Berlin in 1936. Dr. Naismith, then seventy-five years old, was sent to those games by the National Association of Basketball Coaches and awarded the first medals. When the game was introduced in the world's greatest amateur sports spectacle, the Olympics, its popularity throughout the world was ensured.

TOURNAMENTS

Tournament play at the high school and college levels resulted in greater exposure for players and teams, which created increased interest in the sport. The National Association of Intercollegiate Athletics (NAIA) and the National Invitation Tournament (NIT) began in 1937. In 1939 the **National Collegiate Athletic Association (NCAA)** and the National Association of Basketball Coaches (NABC) sponsored their first national tournament, which eventually developed into the "Final Four." High schools also developed tournaments at the state and even the national levels in the 1930s. Tournament play has become so popular that the time during the national tournaments is referred to by sports fans as "March Madness."

CHANGES THROUGH THE DECADES

Most developments in how basketball was played resulted in continued expansion of the game. The 1930s, when the sport spread throughout the country and awareness increased, was called the "Golden Era of Basketball." Intersectional college play took place as well as the expansion of professional basketball, which started in the early 1900s. Coaching and the resultant planning by coaches and athletic administrators also fostered this expansion.

During the 1940s, when World War II forced sports to develop in and out of the military effort, basketball saw an *offensive* explosion. The primary causes were the advent of the jump shot and the coaches focus on revolutionary team offenses, including the fast break. Also, in 1946 the National Basketball Association (NBA) started as the major professional basketball league.

The imbalance that favored offense and scoring was followed by the 1950s when coaches developed all forms of *defensive* schemes to blunt a team's scoring efforts. This included different levels of defense from halfcourt to fullcourt, various forms of pressure defense designed to upset offensive rhythm, and different combinations of defense (player-to-player, zone, and variations of both).

The 1960s brought offensive and defensive *balance* and stability to the game and tremendous improvements in individual player development. This was because of basketball becoming more specialized, summer basketball camps, and improved coaching.

The popularity of television impacted the sport in the 1970s as the *technology* era began. Huge arenas, televised college and professional games, and technical coaching became commonplace at all levels of basketball. Even so, as late as 1980 CBS Television showed the Final Four on tape delay. However, during the 1980s basketball truly became *international* and the United States dominated the sport in the Olympics.

BASKETBALL TODAY

Modern basketball remains the same basic game Naismith invented over one hundred years ago. But it has become a game for everyone—large and small, young and old, men and women, in school and out of school and able-bodied as well as physically challenged players.

Basketball has become the most popular participation sport in American schools and the most popular team sport throughout the world with over two hundred countries participating. It is also a popular spectator sport; the Final Four and NBA games are televised around the world.

▶ **National Collegiate Athletic Association (NCAA)**
In 1939, the NCAA along with the National Association of Basketball Coaches (NABC) sponsored their first national basketball tournament, which eventually developed into the "Final Four."

6 BASKETBALL

A uniqueness of the sport is the myriad of ways the game has been modified. Basketball can be played for competition or recreation, 5-on-5 fullcourt down to 4-on-4, 3-on-3, 2-on-2, or 1-on-1 halfcourt. Three-on-three tournaments are widespread. Individualized competitions and shooting contests are also common. These various forms of halfcourt basketball are called "hunch" or "ratball" and have become the foundation for building the deep understanding of the sport that players and spectators have developed.

SUMMARY

- Basketball was originally invented as an indoor recreation sport, but has become a game with worldwide appeal, both indoors and outdoors, as a competitive sport.
- James Naismith invented this American team sport in 1892.
- Basketball is played on a rectangular court with two elevated horizontal baskets.
- The purpose of basketball is to put the ball in your basket (offense) while preventing the other team from putting the ball in their basket (defense).
- The team "keepaway" game of basketball has attained worldwide popularity because of its flexibility and universal appeal.

THE **FACILITIES** AND **EQUIPMENT:** VITAL TO THE GAME

OBJECTIVES

After reading this chapter, you should be able to:

- Describe the basic facility needed for basketball.
- Describe equipment for basketball.

KEY TERMS

While reading this chapter, you will become familiar with the following terms:

- ▶ Defense
- ▶ Endlines
- ▶ Offense
- ▶ Playground Basketball
- ▶ Shot
- ▶ Sidelines

The Essentials for Basketball

A ball and basket on a basketball court, combined with socks, shoes, shorts and shirt are the essentials to practice or play the game.

A basketball game is a timed contest between two teams of five players each plus substitutes. It may be played on an informal basis by reducing the size of the playing area (court) in half and using less than five players per team (1-on-1, 2-on-2, 3-on-3, or 4-on-4), but is formally played on a fullcourt.

Halfcourt Basketball is an organization whose purpose is to promote and organize the three-on-three game across the United States. They have developed a complete set of rules and guidelines for league play. Three-on-three competitions are held in major cities all over the country.

COURT

The boundary area where a game is played is a rectangular basketball court that has an official size of fifty feet wide by eighty-four feet (secondary schools) or ninety-four feet (college or professional) long. The basketball court is usually an indoor arena but may be located outdoors. The floor is usually a hard wood or synthetic surface. The area within the rectangle is called *in bounds* (inside the playing area), while the territory outside of this rectangle is called *out of bounds*. The court's "length" boundaries are called **sidelines** and the "width" boundaries are termed **endlines** or **baselines**.

FIGURE 2-1 The ball.

THE BALL

The game is played with a round, inflated, bounceable ball that is 29–30 inches around, from 20–22 ounces in weight, and inflated with 7–9 pounds of air pressure for men's basketball (Figure 2-1). These qualities were developed to ensure uniformity of the game. Similar standards have been developed for women's basketball—27–29 inches around, 18–20 ounces in weight, and 6-8 pounds of air pressure. The ball is molded from leather or composition materials. Actually, a smaller ball should be used before grade 7 (ages 11–12), and even high school and college basketball for women has a smaller ball for their game. For play on outdoor courts, a rubber or composition ball should be used because of the high degree of wear of the ball when it is used on asphalt and concrete surfaces, common materials on outdoor courts.

BASKET

The object of the game is to score points by shooting the ball through the elevated *basket* (ring or hoop). An attempt to score by throwing the basketball through the hoop is called a **shot.** The team with the most points at the end of the game is the winner. A team is on **offense** when attempting to score at their basket and on **defense** when preventing the other team from scoring at the opposite end of the court. The basket hoop is a metal ring eighteen inches in diameter suspended ten feet above the floor; basket hoops are at both ends of the court. Although an elevated basket appears small, two basketballs can pass simultaneously through the basket ring. Informal *pickup games,* sometimes called *hunch, ratball,* or **playground basketball** are most often played to a given number of baskets or points rather than a specified amount of time.

BACKBOARD

Each basket ring is attached to a fan-shaped or rectangular backboard perpendicular to the court, parallel to the baseline, and at equal distances from the sidelines. The backboard is four feet inside the endline. Backboards are made of wood, plastic, metal, and glass. Transparent glass backboards were developed to allow those spectators seated behind the basket to see through them; these backboards break easier than other types. They must be installed and maintained properly to

▶ **Sidelines**
The basketball court's length boundaries.

▶ **Endlines**
Also referred as the baselines, these are the width boundaries.

▶ **Shot**
An attempt to serve by throwing the basketball through the hoop.

▶ **Offense**
The team attempting to score a basket at their end of the court.

▶ **Defense**
Preventing the other team from scoring at the opposite end of the court.

▶ **Playground Basketball**
May be referred to as pickup games, hunch, or ratball; informal games often played to a given number of points as opposed to a timed contest.

prevent shattering. The backboards are designed for "banking" shots into the basket and to deflect inaccurate shots back onto the court.

CLOTHING

Personal equipment such as basketball shoes and socks are important for playing basketball. Clean, well-fitted socks (two pair are recommended) should be carefully put on "from the toe to the ankle" to ensure that no wrinkles are present. A wrinkle is a potential friction "hotspot" that is likely to produce a blister. The shoes should fit comfortably and be made specifically for basketball. The laces should be tightened snugly and individually from the toe to the ankle. It is reversed when the shoes are removed. Be sure they are "aired out" to dry naturally when not being used. A basketball uniform consists of shorts and a shirt or jersey. These should be lightweight to allow free circulation and body ventilation.

SUMMARY:

- Indoor basketball courts are rectangular areas made of wood or synthetic materials.
- Various sizes of basketballs are used to make shot attempts or goal throws at elevated basket rings.
- Vertical backboards are placed behind the basket to bank shots into the basket.
- Properly fitted socks, shoes, shorts and shirts are needed to practice and play the game.

CHAPTER 3

RULES AND REGULATIONS OF
BASKETBALL

OBJECTIVES

After reading this chapter, you should be able to:

- Describe the basic rules for playing and officiating basketball.
- Apply the informal regulations for playing recreational basketball.
- Know that there were thirteen original rules.
- State ballhandling rules.
- Understand timing and scoring rules.
- Know basic fouls and penalties.

KEY TERMS

While reading this chapter, you will become familiar with the following terms:

- ► Dribbling
- ► Federation Rules
- ► Foul
- ► Officials

- ► Pivot Foot
- ► Rebound
- ► Traveling
- ► Turnover

PLAYING AND OFFICIATING

Playground basketball is the game in its purest form with fun and recreation as the purpose behind playing. The game thrives there without regard to fans, coaches, referees, or time. Yet even in an informal game there is acknowledgment of and respect for the rules of the game. Without the rules there is no game. They set limits and ensure fairness; rules provide law and order for any game, including basketball.

The pick up game of basketball is a unique happening in American sports. Basketball players think nothing of showing up on a court and expecting a contest to materialize. And it usually does whether 1-on-1, 2-on-2, 3-on-3, or a full 5-on-5. With little organization and no scheduling, heated competition springs up around hoops across America. Although players on the court have not read the official rule book, they usually know the game and give it identity by playing by the rules and forging their own informal regulations. You will be a part of this process.

Rules also keep the game under control. Basketball is somewhat dishonest with itself when it claims to be a noncontact sport while actually allowing much physical contact. This causes the game to weave and wobble along on its way like an untrue tire. In reality, basketball games do have physical contact, especially in defense. Pushing, holding your ground, and giving nothing without a battle is evidence of heated competition.

However, too much contact can and will destroy a game. Muscle will win over skill and the game becomes unfair. Pickup players must call their own fouls and keep the game fair by applying the rules. When you are muscled out of a skill play, you need to call a foul. Announce your judgment that a player fouled you. The opponents may disagree, but will accept the call. They realize the rules must be followed to have a game.

Pick up, or playground, basketball games are more open to lax rules than organized games with officials. You should seldom make calls that stop the flow of the game. Getting into the feel of the game is more important than winning and losing. In general, the code of pick up games is a no-harm/no-foul philosophy.

Resentment tends to build in a competitive game, then the rules are bent, stretched, and even ignored at times. It is always best to give the opponent the benefit of the doubt and make only necessary calls during pick up games. The underlying respect for the rules will keep the game basically fair. Remember, respect your opponents and the game by applying the rules to keep the game fair.

Organized basketball games need several elements to ensure fairness and good competition: skilled players to *play* the game; knowledgeable coaches to *coach* the game; and, respected officials to *enforce the rules* of the game.

The **officials** that enforce the rules are the *scorer*, who keeps the official scorebook with points, fouls, timeouts, and running score; the *timer*, who starts and stops the official clock; and the *floor officials* (two or three of them per game), the court enforcers on the floor. They blow their whistles on rule infractions and hand down the appropriate awards and punishments on each judgment call. Basketball is one of the most difficult games in the world to officiate. Calls are made—some right and some wrong. The officials are only attempting to make it an even contest—consistent and fair for both teams.

Sources for the Rules

- Elementary through high school for boys and girls—Federation:
    National Federation of State High School Associations
    11724 Plaza Circle, Box 20626
    Kansas City, MO 64195
- College (Men)-National Collegiate Athletic Association (NCAA),
  National Association of Intercollegiate Athletics (NAIA), and National
  Junior College Athletic Association (NJCAA):
    National Collegiate Athletic Association
    Publishing Department, P.O. Box 1906
    Overland Park, KS 66211-2422
- Amateur-Olympic or Federation of International Basketball
  Associations (FIBA):
    USA Basketball   or   FIBA
    1750 E. Boulder Street   P.O. Box 70 06 07
    Colorado Springs, CO 80909   Kislterhofstrasse 16
        W-800 Munchen 70
        Federal Rep. of Germany
- Professional-National Basketball Association (NBA):
    The Sporting News
    P.O. Box 56
    St. Louis, MO 63166

Respect the officials whose job it is to uphold those rules. Coaches and players should also know the rules as well as the officials who enforce them. If you understand the rules, you will understand the game and realize how tough it is to officiate. All you can expect is for the officials to officiate or "call" the game consistently. It is the responsibility of players to adjust to the official's enforcement of the rules during each game and to share the responsibility for enforcing the rules.

There are several sets of rules used in basketball. The primary ones used for most elementary and secondary school play are the **Federation rules** for both boys and girls.

▶ **Officials**
Those who enforce the rules during a basketball game. Officials include the scorer, the timer, and the floor officials.

▶ **Federation Rules**
The primary rules used for most elementary and secondary school play.

THE ORIGINAL RULES

From the original list of thirteen rules came the basketball rules of today. Most of those rules have been retained. The first three rules allowed the ball to be thrown in any direction with one or both hands; allowed the ball to be batted in any direction with one or both hands (never with the fist), now called the dribble; and prohibited a player from running with the ball. Rule number four prevented a player from holding the ball against their body, which is allowed today. This rule, to reduce rough play, has been replaced by the *held ball* (jump ball) rule. Rule five stated that "no shouldering, holding, pushing, tripping, or striking the person of an opponent shall be allowed" and was the primary rough play rule. Number six defined certain infractions or violations as personal fouls. Today the penalty isn't as severe. Naismith's seventh rule gave points to an opponent when three consecutive fouls were made. Today a team must earn its own points. Rule number eight, the basket scoring rule, has stood the test of time with the addition of "goaltending" and "basket interference" sections. When the ball goes out of bounds, it originally went to the team who got there first. Now it is awarded to the opponents of the team that caused the ball to go out of bounds. In rules ten and eleven, a referee was identified. The first code of rules provided for a game of two fifteen-minute halves with five minutes rest between, as rule number twelve indicated. The final rule, thirteen, provided that the team scoring the most goals was the winner.

An overwhelming majority of basketball rules have been retained over the years. Presently, the guidelines for rules are designed to ensure fair play (no one is to be put at a disadvantage), balance (between offense and defense), safety (the players' welfare is uppermost), work-ability (practical), continuity (the action must flow), and no profit from infraction.

BALLHANDLING

Ball movement in basketball must take place by passing (throwing the ball to another player) or **dribbling** (bouncing the ball continuously on the court surface with one hand. A pass can bounce any number of times (bounce pass) or travel directly from player to player without touching the court surface (air pass). The ball cannot be carried, struck with the fist, or *intentionally* kicked.

A team is said to be on *offense* when in possession of the ball while the opposing team is said to be on *defense*. Team possession changes constantly during the course of a game. Defensive players (defenders) try to prevent the offensive players from scoring by forcing them to take forced shots or even to *block* their shots. Defenders also attempt to gain ball possession by intercepting a pass or taking the ball away on the dribble (referred to as stealing the ball). The defender is not allowed to hold, strike, push, trip, or impede the progress of the offensive player.

A ballhandler (a player who possesses the ball) cannot move from one spot to another without *dribbling*. A violation of this rule is called **traveling.** Traveling is carrying the ball or walking with the ball. The penalty for this is the awarding of the ball to the opponent.

Another ballhandling violation is called a *double-dribble*. It occurs when a player dribbling the ball touches it more than once per bounce or touches it with both hands at once. A player must either pass or shoot at the end of a dribble move; to dribble again would be a double-dribble violation.

A ballhandler not dribbling must establish one foot in one spot on the floor (although it may pivot or rotate on that spot). The establishment of this **pivot foot** allows the player to step with the other foot in any direction any number of times. In Figure 3-1, the pivot foot is shown as the left foot (either foot may be used). On a legal dribble, the ball must leave the dribbler's hand before the pivot foot is lifted. When stopping, the first foot that hits the court is the pivot foot. If a player lands on both feet at once, either foot may be used as a pivot foot (Figure 3-2).

FIGURE 3-1A Left foot, pivot foot (start).

FIGURE 3-1B Left foot, pivot foot (finish).

▶ **Dribbling**

Bouncing the ball continuously on the court surface with one hand.

▶ **Traveling**

A dribbling violation when a player carries the ball or walks with the ball without dribbling.

▶ **Pivot Foot**

A ballhandler who is not dribbling must establish one foot in one spot on the floor and may pivot or rotate on that spot.

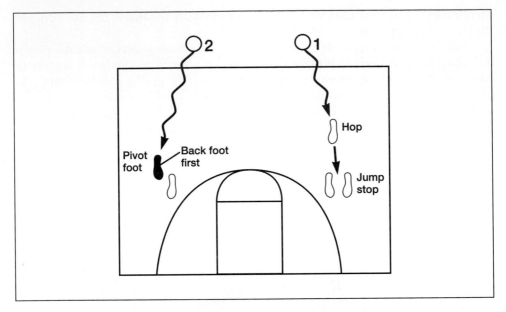

FIGURE 3-2 Pivot foot—stride stop; pivot foot—jump stop.

TIMING

As stated previously, the length of an official basketball game ranges from twenty-four minutes for elementary/junior high school to thirty-two minutes at the secondary level and forty minutes in college. The professional game consists of four twelve-minute periods. All other levels have games in four *quarters*, except for college play, divided into two twenty-minute halves. A timing device controls a scoreboard, where the time and score are readily displayed for officials, players, and spectators. The intermission between halves of a game is called *halftime* and usually lasts fifteen minutes (ten minutes in secondary schools). In games played in quarters, there is a one-minute time period between the first and second quarters and the third and fourth quarters. If the score is tied at the end of a regulation game, added *overtime* of five minutes is played until a winner is determined. If at the end of one overtime the score is still tied, another five-minute period is played. This continues until one team wins. A *shot clock* is used at many levels of organized play to limit the time a team may have the ball during an offensive possession. For example, college basketball has a thirty-second clock for the women's game and a thirty-five-second clock for men's basketball. Professional basketball uses a twenty-four-second shot clock.

FIGURE 3-3b A held ball situation—center jumps.

FIGURE 3-3a A held ball situation two players in possession of the ball.

A team may stop play by calling a timeout. A coach or player must signal to a floor official, who stops play for a timeout that is usually one minute long. The timeout signal is made by forming a "T" with his hands or sometimes a closed fist is used. A timeout is usually requested to come up with new strategies or change the flow of a game. Officials may take a timeout player injury, eyeglass lens problem, a correctable error situation (scoring/timing mistake), or to replace a disqualified player.

The game clock starts on the opening jump (or side out). From that point, it stops whenever play stops except after a field goal. The clock stops whenever a floor official blows the whistle—for violations, fouls, and jump balls. The game clock begins whenever the ball is put in play. For an inbound pass, the clock starts when the ball first touches a player inbounds. On a missed free throw (a special penalty shot), the clock starts when it is legally tapped. The three ways of putting the ball in play are an inbound pass, a missed free throw, and a held ball or jump ball situation. This third method involves two opposing players trying to tap the ball with a hand to a teammate as the ball is tossed into the air between them by an official (Figure 3-3). A *jump ball* occurs to start a period of play, in a double foul situation (on the ball), when two opponents gain ball possession at the same time, in the case of the ball being lodged between the basket and backboard, and when the ball goes out of bounds after touching two opposing players at once. At most levels of play, held ball situations result in alternate awarding of the ball out-of-bounds. This is also the violation in men's college play when a closely guarded player—within six feet to the ballhandler—holds the ball or dribbles the ball for five seconds.

The *midcourt* line (or half line) runs from sideline to sideline through the exact middle of the court. This line is also called the ten-second line because a team that inbounds the ball in its backcourt (men's basketball) has ten seconds to advance the ball into its front court. It is a *backcourt* violation if that team returns the ball to the backcourt after entering the front court near their basket.

Other time violations occur if a team cannot inbound the ball within five seconds, if any offensive player spends more than three seconds in his offensive free throw lane, or when an offensive player with the ball is closely guarded by a defender for five seconds in certain situations (high school or college).

SCORING

A successful shot taken during game action is a *field goal* (or basket). If the shooter made the shot, two points would be added to the team's score unless the shooter took the shot behind the three-point arc, then three points would be added to the score. The ball can be shot upward, tapped upward (a tap or tip-in), or thrown down through the hoop (also referred to as a dunk, slam, or stuff), but the ball must pass downward through the basket. If time runs out while the ball is in flight, the shot counts as a field goal.

After a field goal, the opponent is awarded *possession* of the ball (team possession). The ball also changes when the offensive team commits a violation, when the ball goes out-of-bounds by the offense, or when an alternating held ball situation occurs.

A missed shot that bounces back toward the court from the basket or backboard is called a **rebound**. Catching a rebound is called *rebounding*, an important method of gaining ball possession.

Losing ball possession by a team creates a **turnover**.

Goaltending is a violation that occurs during a shot attempt. It happens when a defender blocks a shot that is going toward the basket, when a defender interferes with the ball or basket while the ball is touching the basket, or when a defender touches the ball while it is in the imaginary cylinder above the basket ring. The penalty for goaltending is to count the shot attempt as a made field goal.

It is also a violation for an offensive player to interfere with the ball or basket while the ball is touching the basket or is in the cylinder—called offensive *interference*. The penalty is loss of possession and also wiping out the possible field goal.

Free throws are special penalty shots that count as a score of one point. They are taken with play stopped and no defense of the shot, from behind the *free throw line* (or foul line). Free throw shooters or foul shooters stand behind the foul line, nineteen feet from the baseline. Free throws are awarded as penalties for a variety of infractions called *fouls*.

FOULS AND PENALTIES

It is against the rules for any player to hold, push, strike, or trip an opponent. These infractions are called personal **fouls** (each player is entitled to only five per game before removal or disqualification).

A personal foul committed by an offensive player with the ball is termed a *player control foul*. The penalty is loss of ball possession. Infractions by a team or player while the clock is stopped are classified as technical fouls. Delay of game, unsportsmanlike conduct, substitution violations, and coach-player conduct problems also are *technical fouls*.

The penalty for a foul is usually one plus one—a bonus shot if the first free throw is made. The bonus occurs in a penalty situation. One free throw is awarded when an offensive player is fouled while shooting and the field goal is made. Two shots are awarded on a foul from a two-point field goal attempt that is missed, and three shots are awarded on a foul from a three-point field goal attempt.

OPPOSING TEAMS

The home team is the host where the game is played, with the opponent called the visiting team. The visiting team gets the basket opposite its bench to start the game, with the teams switching baskets for the second half.

The officials enforce the rules, the boundaries of the game. The floor officials are the referees who apply the rules and make the calls on the court while the game is in progress. They stop action by using whistles when they make a ruling (call). As stated earlier, the officials apply the rules to keep the game within boundaries of play and must make many judgment calls to ensure fairness. Players, coaches, and officials are responsible for actively enforcing the rules.

SUMMARY

- Rules of basketball are necessary to define the boundaries of the game, set the limits, and to ensure fair play.
- The rules and regulations of competition and recreational basketball keep the game under control.
- In organized competition games, officials are designated to enforce the rules of the game.
- A ballhandler must not walk with the ball otherwise a traveling violation will be called and the ball possession goes to the opposing team.
- All levels of the game have specified periods or quarters with an intermission in the middle of the game.
- After a successful field goal the opposing team gets possession of the basketball.
- Each player is allowed five personal fouls per game.

▶ **Rebound**
A missed shot that bounces back toward the court from the basket or backboard.

▶ **Turnover**
Losing a ball possession by a team.

▶ **Foul**
An infraction of the rules when a player holds, pushes, strikes, or trips an opponent.

CHAPTER 4

MOVEMENTS ON THE COURT: BASICS

OBJECTIVES

After reading this chapter, you should be able to:

- Know and demonstrate the basketball position or ready position.
- Understand the staggered stance and parallel stance.
- Carry out the basic starts—forward, sideward, and backward.
- Perform the basic steps of movement—change of speed and direction, moves, and turns or pivots.
- Perform the jumps needed in basketball—two-foot, one-foot, and quick jumps.
- Execute the two basic stops—jump and stride.

KEY TERMS

While reading this chapter, you will become familiar with the following terms:

- ► Basketball Position
- ► Jump Stop
- ► Parallel Stance
- ► Staggered Stance
- ► Stride Stop

Movement magic

Movement skills are the fundamentals for learning to control your body. This includes basic stance or positions and movements that allow you to play basketball at your best. *Stance, starts, steps, stops* and *jumps*, comprise movement magic.

STANCE

The basic stance in basketball is called the **basketball** or **ready position** (BP)(Figure 4-1). This position best prepares you for all situations on offense and defense. It is a stance of balance and quickness that is especially important when changes in body position or quick movements are required. On offense it is called a "triple threat" position when you have the ball; (i.e., ready to pass, shoot, or drive).

Basketball stance consists of a recommended foot placement called the **staggered stance,** as shown in Figure 4-2a. Your feet are about shoulder width apart and in a heel-to-toe rela-

FIGURE 4-1 Ready position—the offense is in the triple threat position. The defense is in a quick stance.

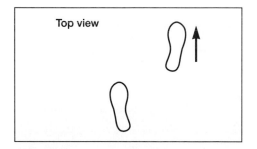

FIGURE 4-2A The staggered stance—heel-and-toe relationship, feet width apart.

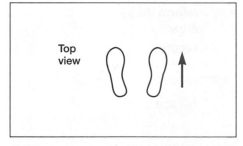

FIGURE 4-2B The parallel stance—toe and-toe relationship, feet shoulder width apart.

▶ **Basketball Position**
The basic stance in basketball that prepares a player in all offensive and defensive situations.

▶ **Staggered Stance**
When a player's feet are shoulder width apart and in a heel-to-toe relationship from front-to-back.

tionship from front-to-back. Either foot may be forward. The staggered stance is the quickest position for movement in all directions. A **parallel stance,** as shown in Figure 4-2b, should be used if you are primarily concerned with side-to-side (lateral) movement or lateral balance, as in jump shooting. This stance is often used when you are a ballhandler catching and stopping or dribbling and stopping (Figure 4-3) or you are a defender moving laterally. Both stances have a slight "toe out" position.

Your body weight should be evenly distributed from side-to-side, front-to-back, and equally on each foot. Be sure your heels are down, with most of the weight on the balls of the feet, but feeling pressure on your heels and toes. Remember, the heels are down and the toes are curled into the floor in the "eagle claw" position.

When you are on defense, you need to also keep your feet active and in constant motion without leaving the floor surface. This activates your leg muscles for quick movement and makes you ready for action.

The head is a key to balance because of its size, location, and role as your balance center (the inner ear). It should be kept at the center of the foot support base. Keep it at the apex of the side-to-side triangle and centered from front-to-back (Figure 4-4a). Your trunk position, also seen in Figure 4-3a, is slightly forward of vertical with the shoulders back and head up and centered.

Your arms and legs should be flexed or bent at the ankle, knee, hip, shoulder, elbow, and wrist joints. The hands and arms are bent and kept close to the body for balance and quickness. The bottom of your whole foot should touch the floor. Get in and stay in your stance. The angle at the knee joint in back of the legs should be 90°–120° (Figure 4-4b).

STARTS

After you are able to get in a stance and stay in a stance, your next motion

FIGURE 4-3A Parallel stance and step. One foot hop.

FIGURE 4-3B Parallel stance. Jump stop triple threat.

FIGURE 4-4A The head is the key to balance—a frontal view.

FIGURE 4-4B Side view—the knees are bent from 90 to 120 degree angles.

task is to *start* quickly. Basketball is a game of quickness (starts, steps, and stops) and balance (stance). You must learn to use your quickness at the right time. This quickness is partially dependent on your inherited abilities but also is based on your learning to think and become quick.

The basketball position is your ready position for a quick start. Get down, stay down, and be ready to start. Move the *line of gravity* near the edge of the base in the desired direction of movement. You can do this by leaning (moving the head) in that direction. The line of gravity is a vertical line through the weight center of the body. For example, Figure 4-5a & b shows the line of gravity moved near the front edge to move forward and near the left side to move left by leading with the head.

For quick starts and steps, you should keep your feet as close to the floor as possible and in contact with the floor most of the time.

Always step first with the foot in the direction of your start. When moving forward, step first with the front foot. When moving to the right, lead with your right foot. Remember, lead foot first. Stay low and pump your arms as you start.

STEPS

The three basic "steps" you will use in basketball are running steps, sliding steps, and turning (or pivoting) steps. Running steps are used

▶ **Parallel Stance**
A side-to-side (lateral) movement often used by a ball handler catching and stopping or dribbling and stopping.

FIGURE 4-5A Move forward—lean forward.

FIGURE 4-5B Move left—lean left.

more on offense, sliding steps on defense, and turning steps on both offense and defense.

Running steps are used with changes of speed and changes of direction while staying close to the floor. Your body should be leaning forward as you run. Also bend your elbows as you pump your arms. You should also learn to start backwards and run backwards on offense or defense. This allows you to maintain vision as you move backwards.

On defense, starts and steps are more of a sliding motion. Keep your feet wide for balance and quickness. These short, quick shuffle steps are taken after starting with the first step in the direction of movement. That first step is taken by pointing the toe in the desired direction, taking a short first step as you push from the back foot and then slide it in the same direction. This is called *step-slide,* as you point the lead foot, take a short *step* in a desired direction followed by a *slide* step with the back foot (Figure 4-6). You need to learn defensive step-slide movements forward, backward, side-to-side, and diagonally.

The defensive step-slide keeps you close to the floor. When done properly your head stays in a level horizontal plane as you move. No bouncing; stay in your stance. Avoid the "bunny hop" move when you slide.

Other step variations include: *stutter steps*—short, choppy steps, used just before a change-of-direction; *change-of-pace*—usually a slow-fast running motion, to produce a burst of speed and be quick at the right time; *change-of-direction*—a move you can use to evade an opponent and make a "zigzag" move (up to 90° change) or a complete reverse change (180°) to go in the opposite direction.

The zigzag move is done by putting your weight on the foot opposite of the way you want to go (plant your foot), point your opposite foot the way you want to go

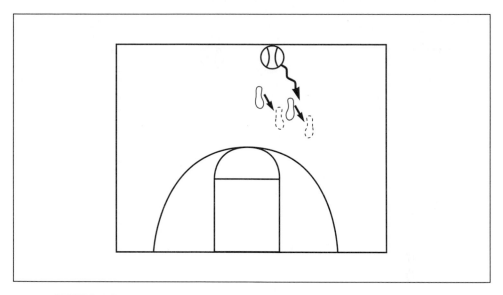

FIGURE 4-6 Point and step with the left foot and slide the right foot.

and push from your plant foot to step in a new direction (point and step). This is a slow-quick move, "slow" as you plant and "quick" as you point and step. It is used on offense or defense.

The 180° reverse is used with a stride or two-count stop (described later). As you land on your back foot first, your weight is over that foot as your front foot hits. Use a double pivot to face in the opposite direction and start with the new front foot. You should be able to reverse with either foot forward.

When starting and stepping, move in straight lines. This allows you to conserve time and space.

TURNS

When you stay in the ready position, make quick starts and steps. Another tool for this purpose is the turn or pivot—a movement that allows you to stay balanced and move quickly by changing direction (Figure 4-7).

Turning or pivoting rotates the body around the ball of one foot while staying in a stance as shown in Figure 4-8. The pivot is a basic skill you can use to change direction and stay in a balanced position. It is used on offense or defense.

Pivoting can be done with either foot and is the center of rotation. A *front turn* is moving the front of the body forward around the pivot foot and a *rear turn* rotates the body in the opposite direction. Both pivots are illustrated in Figures 4-9a-d.

Offensively, you can use a pivot with or without the ball. On defense, a pivot is one of the basic starting moves used when changing directions. Defensive rebounding usually requires the use of a pivot.

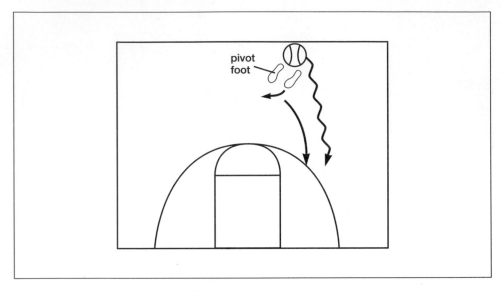

FIGURE 4-7 Pivot or turn.

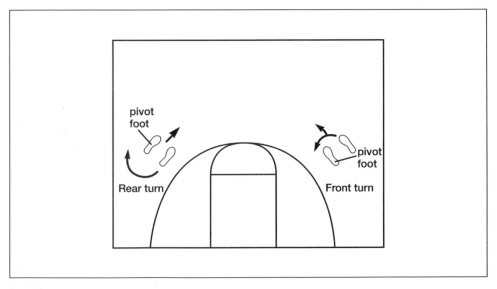

FIGURE 4-8 Pivot or turn—rotating the body around one foot while staying in BP.

The basic pivoting principles are: stay in your stance, keep your head level; keep your feet wide (shoulder width); maintain balance with your head up; pivot quickly and properly; use front or rear turns to rotate up to 180°. Pivots are usually one-quarter to one-half turns.

FIGURE 4-9A Pivots—a front turn; right foot starts.

FIGURE 4-9B Pivots—front turn; right foot ends.

FIGURE 4-9C Pivots—rear turns; right foot starts.

FIGURE 4-9D Pivots—rear turn on the right foot.

STOPS

Being quick with balance allows you to stay in your stance, start and step quickly, and stop quickly in a balanced position.

The two stops you should master are the **jump stop** (the basic tool for stopping on offense and defense), and the **stride stop** (used when running at full speed).

The jump stop, as seen in Figure 4-10, is a one-count movement. It is executed by hopping slightly from one foot, skimming close to the floor, and landing on both feet simultaneously in a parallel or staggered stance. This stop is preferred because it conserves time and space; can be used on offense (with or without the ball) or defense; is a close companion to the pivot; can be used to get in a quick ready position for shooting (dominant foot forward), passing, or dribbling and, finally, at the end of a dribble or when receiving a pass to attain body control and balance.

You can use the *stride stop* or two-count stop when moving at faster speeds or when reversing directions. You should land on the rear foot (first count), followed closely by the front foot (second count) as shown in Figure 4-11. When using the stride stop with the ball at the end of a dribble, the back foot is defined in the rules as the pivot foot.

JUMPS

Jumping is an important skill for rebounding, shooting, catching, and other ball-handling tasks. One-footed jumps are used when shooting a layin on a drive move or blocking a shot. This jump takes time and space, but you can jump higher

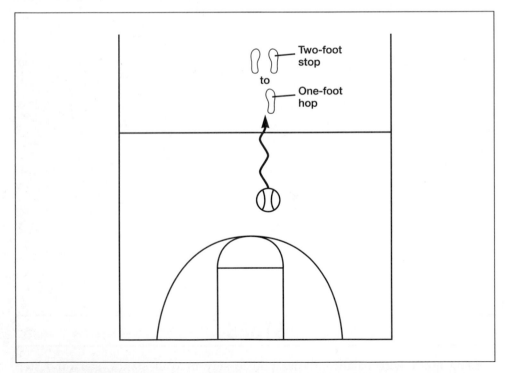

FIGURE 4-10 Jump (quick) stop. From a one-foot hop, skim to a two foot stop.

because of your movement momentum. The danger is losing body control and causing a foul or collision with an opposing player. It is tough to land with balance and control after a one-foot jump. Your technique should emphasize a hard foot *plant* on your jumping foot, high *knee action* with the opposite leg, and arm up on the same side as the "high knee" (Figure 4-12).

Two-footed jumps are slower but stronger jumps, taken in congested areas (rebounding, power layin). You should usually rebound from the basketball position using two hands and two feet (Figure 4-13).

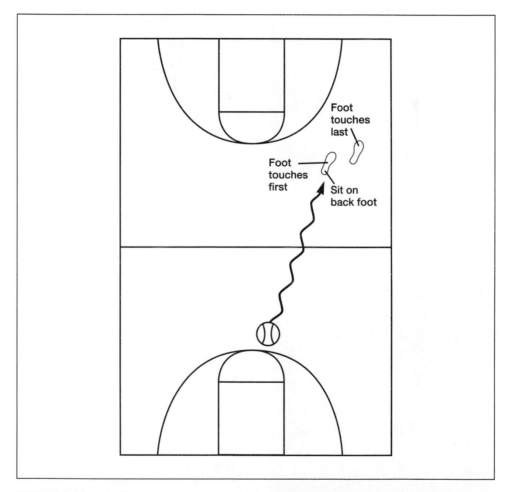

FIGURE 4-11 Stride stop—a two-count stop. Sit on the back foot to regain balance.

▶ **Jump Stop**

The basic tool for stopping on offense and defense.

▶ **Stride Stop**

A stop used when running at full speed.

FIGURE 4-12A One-foot jump—start of a lay-up.

FIGURE 4-12B One-foot jump—end of a lay-up.

FIGURE 4-13 Two-foot jump to rebound.

The best jump for combining body position and control with conservation of time and space is the *quick jump*. This is a two feet, two hands jump without momentum in traffic. The basics of this jump are: start with arms up in ready position; bring arms down slightly to gather and build momentum; and perform a two-hand, two-foot vertical jump landing in BP. Figure 4-14 shows this three-part sequence.

SUMMARY

- The basketball position has both your feet on the floor, weight evenly distributed from front-to-back and side-to-side, and your head in the apex of the balance triangle.

FIGURE 4-14B Quick jump. The arms should be up.

FIGURE 4-14B Two-hands, two-feet. Land and protect the ball.

- Although you have the options of a parallel or staggered stance, you always come back to the basic ready position.
- Starts are made with the lead foot into the steps of motion, changes of speed and direction (stutter steps, zigzags, reverses, and pivots).
- Pivots may be front or rear turns.
- Jumps are used in basketball to rebound, shoot, and catch the ball.
- The jump stop is the basic stop in basketball and is used in most fundamental skills, while the stride stop is used when moving at high speed.

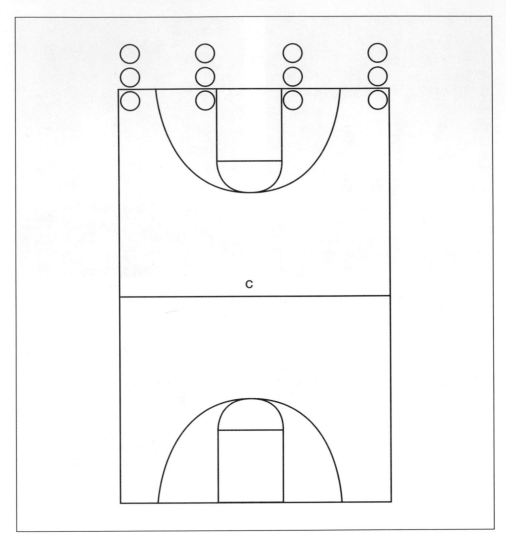

FIGURE 4-15 Line drill.

Assessment 4-1

The Line Drill

Name   Section   Date

Description:

The basic drill for learning the basketball basics is called the line drill. You can do it alone or it can be performed in three or four lines, as shown in Figure 4-15. Line drill reminders include: each fundamental skill variation is done for one circuit (down and back); the first player in each line should always come to basketball position on the baseline—be ready before you are required to start and move. You need to listen for directions and the starting command; keep equal side-to-side spacing; as a group of four reaches the free throw lane line, the next group of four should start; all players move to the opposite baseline and reform with the first group of four again in the ready position. A selection of skills and circuits are made for each class or practice and should include all fundamentals on a regular basis.

The line drill variations for this chapter are quick starts, selected moves, and quick stops. Included are: stutter steps (change-of-pace); offensive zigzag (change-of-direction jump stop/rear turns); pivots (front, rear and full or half turns); slow-quick running (follow a designated leader using peripheral vision to stay even); spacing jog (slow-quick)—the first four players begin on command and move down the court with change-of-speed moves, next groups attempting to start and maintain 15–18 foot spacing intervals behind them; one-foot, two-foot, or quick jumps—three consecutive repetitions at the free throw line, half line, opposite free throw-line, and opposite base line.

BASICS OF
BALLHANDLING

OBJECTIVES

After reading this chapter, you should be able to:

- Have a better understanding of dribbling principles.
- Understand the fundamentals of passing.
- Execute fundamentals of catching.

KEY TERMS

While reading this chapter, you will become familiar with the following terms:

- ► Back Dribble
- ► Baseball Pass
- ► Chest Air Pass
- ► Crossover Dribble
- ► Low/High Dribble
- ► Overhead Pass
- ► Push Pass
- ► Spin Dribble

Important Skills

Passing and catching are the most essential team ballhandling skills. Passes should be quick, on target, timed properly and be deceptive. Catch and pass with two hands. Players should learn to control and speed dribble, as well as develop the crossover and spin dribbles, while always seeing the whole court.

Ballhandling encompasses all offensive moves with the basketball—passing, catching, dribbling, shooting, individual moves, and rebounding. For our purposes, this chapter describes ballhandling as including only the skills of passing, catching, and dribbling the basketball.

Passing and catching are the most important of the individual offensive fundamentals with the ball. Shooting will be considered as a pass to the basket. Dribbling is a secondary offensive weapon that should not be misused.

DRIBBLING

Dribbling is a touch skill, not a sight skill. You should learn to dribble, "with vision" up the court, without watching the ball. This can be accomplished by focusing on the offensive basket, while dribbling and seeing the whole floor. Remind yourself to "see the net" at the opposite basket as you dribble.

The dribble is a push-pull motion of the arm, wrist, and fingers as the elbow extends and the wrist and fingers flex. The ball is controlled by the fingers and pads of the hand, so spread your fingers comfortably and keep them cupped. Your hand is a suction cup on the ball. Maintain contact with the ball as much as possible.

Use a jump stop to end the dribble. This stop is the best method for avoiding traveling, while at the same time conserving critical time and space for passing or shooting. It allows either foot to be the pivot foot. (Figure 5-1 illustrates these rules.) The primary objective of dribbling is to create a move that allows you to pass to a teammate for a score. Other acceptable uses are: moving past a defender using the dribble and driving to the basket; getting someone else open; advancing the ball up the court; achieving a better passing angle to a teammate; and, getting out of trouble, such as a trap situation.

Learn to use either hand to dribble. Develop the weak hand, but use the preferred hand whenever possible. Always use the hand away from the defender when you are being closely guarded. In this situation, protect the ball with the body and the opposite hand. Keep the ball low and to the side of the body. Keep tension on the legs whenever a defense player is near; stay in your stance (Figure 5-2). The ball should be low and close to your body, with your elbow in tight, and the ball close to the floor on the protected side.

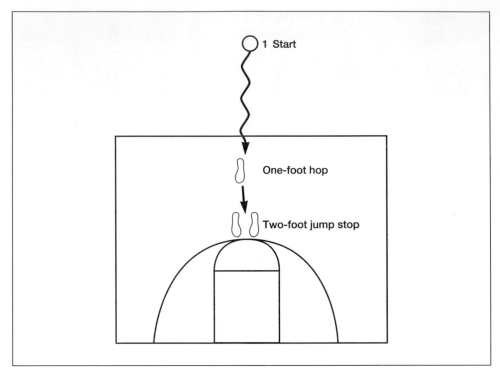

FIGURE 5-1 Ending dribble—jump stop.

When the ball is "put on the floor," as the dribbler, you should be focusing on a point upcourt such as driving to the basket, or going past the defender. Avoid dribbling between two defenders and be alert for defenders setting traps (Figure 5-3).

Use the right dribble at the right time. A control or low dribble should be used around defenders when you are closely guarded. A speed or high dribble can be used in the open court when advancing the ball.

DRIBBLING MOVES

FIGURE 5-2 Low and control dribble.

The control or **low dribble,** as shown in Figure 5-2, requires a staggered stance and begins in ready position with your ball side foot back. Your opposite hand is used for protection from the defender. It cannot be used to push the defender back but only to protect the ball. The basic motion is a sliding movement similar to defensive slides. Massage the ball by keeping it low and protected by the body. The ball is dribbled on the side of your body opposite the defensive player.

When using the speed or **high dribble** (see Figure 5-4), push the ball out in front and go get it. The ball can be dribbled higher, near waist level, to attain more speed. The faster the movement, the farther out front and the higher the ball should be pushed.

The change of pace move is changing speeds, stop, and start. When slowing or stopping, straighten up slightly to relax the defender. This should be used to move past a defender who takes the "slow pace" or "stop" fake.

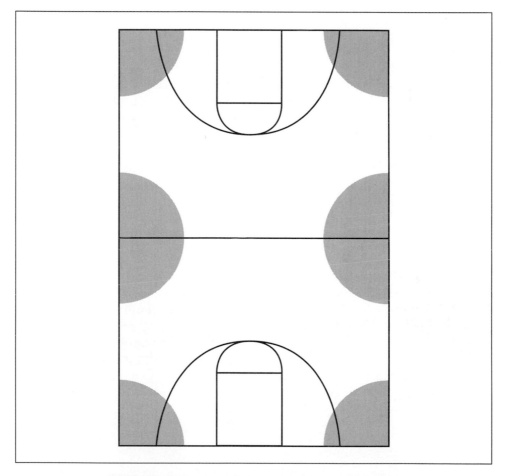

FIGURE 5-3 Stay out of the trap areas on the court.

▶ **Low/High Dribble**

For a low dribble the ball is dribbled on the opposite side of your body from the defensive player. The high dribble can be dribbled higher near the waist to attain more speed.

Performance Tips

- *Always be prepared*—pass first, dribble last, and shoot when open.
- *Give up the ball by passing to the open player*—create the move that allows a pass to a teammate for a score. Look for and create assists.
- *Make the easy pass through or by the defender*—don't gamble on passes. Be neither careless nor overly cautious.
- *The passer and catcher*—should take responsibility for completing the pass. When an incomplete pass is thrown, both the passer and catcher are responsible.
- *The quickest passes are air passes*—the crisp air pass is quicker than the lob pass and the bounce pass. Therefore, the air pass is the primary pass to use. Whenever possible, perimeter passes around the defense should be air passes. Lob passes are good on fast break situations and passing the ball to the low post position.
- *Bounce passes* are used when passing to a post position player or an open backdoor cut.
- *Keep two hands on the ball* until the pass is made. The ball should be held with your fingers spread on both sides of the ball (whole hand on the ball).
- *Fake passes* work well when closely guarded. Make a believable fake to the pass receiver. Use pass fakes to freeze the defense and set up the backdoor.
- *Special situations*—move after a pass is made; never pass across under your defensive basket, as an interception there will result in a score by the opponents; when the pass comes back out on the perimeter from the baseline, look to reverse the ball quickly to the other side of the court; be aware of passing rhythm—an effective pass following infrequent ball movement is a pass thrown immediately (slow-quick); and against a pressure defense it is best to pass sooner.

The **crossover** or switch dribble is used in the open court when there is sufficient room between the dribbler and defender and when the dribbler has momentum to move past the defender, as shown in Figure 5-5. The ball is pushed low and quickly across the body; push the ball from right to left (or vice versa) as a zigzag move from right to left (or vice versa) is made. This move is used when the defender overplays the path of the dribbler on the ball side.

FIGURE 5-4 Speed, or high, dribble.

FIGURE 5-5A Crossover dribble—before crossing.

The **spin dribble** is used for maximum ball protection when you are closely guarded (body is kept between ball and defender, as seen in Figure 5-6a. The disadvantage of this move is that you briefly lose sight of the defenders and teammates. Footwork includes a jump stop and a zigzag move. As the 270° rear turn or pivot is made on the left (or right) foot, the right (left) hand "pulls" the ball with the pivot until the turn is completed and the first step is made with the right (or left) foot. The ball is

FIGURE 5-5B Crossover dribble—after crossing.

kept close to the body. The pull is similar to pulling a pistol from a holster. Pull the ball and keep it tight to avoid the defender's reach or slap around move (Figure 5-6b). After the rear turn is completed, the ball is switched to the opposite hand and full court vision is regained (Figure 5-6c). This move changes direction from an angle that is forward from right to left (or vice versa) as the ball is moved from the right hand to the left hand (or vice versa).

The **back dribble** is used to back away from trouble, defensive traffic, or a trap (Figure 5-7). When dribbling with the right (left) hand, break down into a control dribble position with your left (right) foot forward. Explode back in a sliding

▶ **Crossover Dribble**
Used on the open court when there is sufficient room between the dribbler and defender and when the dribbler has momentum to move past the defender.

▶ **Spin Dribble**
This is used for maximum ball protection when you are closely guarded.

▶ **Back Dribble**
Used to back away from trouble, defensive traffic, or a trap.

FIGURE 5-6A Spin dribble—start low.

FIGURE 5-6B Spin dribble—pull the ball.

FIGURE 5-6C Spin dribble—end, move past defender.

movement to get away from the defense. After re-establishing a gap on the defense, any dribble may be used to penetrate or go by the defender. The crossover dribble is especially effective following the dribble rocker.

The behind-the-back dribble is used to change hands and go past a defender overplaying on the right (left). This is done by changing direction slightly to the left (right) and going by on the dribbler's left (right). As the left (right) foot is moved forward, the ball is moved from right to left (or vice versa) behind the back, coming up under the left (right) hand for a continuation of the dribble. The coordination of the dribble and footwork can be carried out by stationary yo-yo "V" dribbling with one hand, while the opposite foot is forward. When the ball is controlled from front to back it can be moved behind the back as a step is taken.

The between-the-legs dribble helps the ballhandler change the ball from one hand to another. When the ball is being dribbled with the right hand, it can be changed to the left hand with the between-the-legs pass when the left or right foot is forward. Reverse for a left-hand dribble. Keep the ball low and crossover between-the-legs with a quick hard push across. The coordination of the dribble and the footwork can be done by walking forward slowly as the ball is crossed over between-the-legs during each step.

PASSING AND CATCHING

Passing and catching are the most neglected offensive fundamentals in basketball. It is essential to develop these skills for the following reasons: they are common denominators to offensive team success; as a good passer and receiver, you

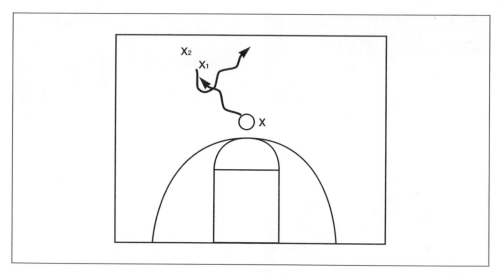

FIGURE 5-7 Back dribble.

have an excellent chance to be an important team member; passing should be the primary weapon of your offensive attack, passing and catching are the quickest ways to move the ball and challenge the defense; and, finally, passing is the most effective way to get the ball to an open player.

BASIC PASSING PRINCIPLES

Good passes must have *quickness*. The pass should be "snappy" and "crisp" but not too hard or too easy. Fred "Tex" Winter, former assistant coach for the Chicago Bulls, refers to the proper sound of a quick pass as a distinct "ping" when it is caught. Therefore, you should put a ping on your pass. Good passes must have a *target* and must be thrown to this specific target. Make every pass perfect. Good passes must have *timing* and must be delivered when the receiver is open (not before and not after).

BASIC PASSES

Chest air pass—the basic air pass for efficient ball movement. The starting position is when the ball is moved from triple threat to the center of your chest close to your body in a "thumbs up" position (Figure 5-8a). When throwing a pass, extend your elbows and pronate your arms (rotate outward) to a "thumbs down" ending position (Figure 5-8b) step with the pass when there is time; and throw the pass toward the out-

▶ **Chest Air Pass**
A basic pass in the air or bounced.

FIGURE 5-8A Chest air pass—start. (thumbs up)

FIGURE 5-8B Chest air pass—end. (thumbs down)

FIGURE 5-8C Chest bounce pass.

side hand or shoulder of the receiver when he/she is moving near a defender.

Chest bounce pass—used primarily for backdoor moves or under a defenders hands (Figure 5-8c). Pass to a target on the floor two-thirds of the way to the receiver. Follow through to that spot on the floor, like a chest air pass to that spot. Throw the pass hard and it should bounce to the receiver's midthigh or waist. Use backspin by pushing your thumbs through the ball, from a thumbs up to thumbs down position. This increases the angle of rebound on the bounce pass to make it easier to handle.

Overhead pass—a valuable pass over the defense as shown in Figure 5-9, especially effective against zone defenses. Keep the ball up, and keep your elbows extended. Throw the pass with your wrists and fingers and keep the ball overhead. Start with your thumbs back, then push your thumbs through the ball, and finally finish with your thumb forward. Your target is "head high" on the receiver.

Baseball pass—used to throw the long pass (as seen in Figure 5-10) for example, over a half court length. Use a stance with your body parallel to the sidelines. Plant your back foot, step with your front foot, and throw the ball by your ear. Carry out a full pronation and extension of the arm and use this pass only with your dominant throwing arm.

One-hand push pass—a quick pass used through or by a closely guarding defender (Figure 5-11). This may be an air or bounce pass. It should be used from the triple threat position and the key is the bent elbow starting position. Pass above or below the defender's arms to find an opening through which to pass. Use vertical fakes and read the defense.

BASIC CATCHING PRINCIPLES

Potential pass receivers should be in basketball position with hands up. Get open and give a target at the right time. Whenever possible the receiver should

FIGURE 5-9A Overhead pass—start.

FIGURE 5-9B Overhead pass—end.

FIGURE 5-10A Baseball pass—start.

FIGURE 5-10B Baseball pass—end.

FIGURE 5-11A One-hand push pass—start.

FIGURE 5-11B One-hand push pass—end.

▶ **Overhead pass**
A valuable pass over the defense.

▶ **Baseball Pass**
Used to throw a long pass such as over a half court length.

▶ **Push Pass**
A quick pass used through or by a closely guarding defender.

FIGURE 5-12 Catch the ball with the feet in the air.

catch the ball with feet in the air (Figure 5-12) and land with a quick stop. This ensures body control, ball possession, and a quick ready position.

The quick stop allows the offensive player to pivot on either foot with a front or rear turn and to face the basket (Figure 5-13). This permits the player with the ball to look and see the whole floor, then decide on the best move to make. Inside players, those close to the basket, should catch and chin the ball with their back to the basket. Let your wrist and elbows give as the pass is caught. This is sometimes called developing "soft hands."

Your eyes should be focused on the pass until it is in your hands. Look the ball into your hands; the ball can't be passed, shot, or dribbled until it is caught. It is also easier to catch the ball when your body is balanced.

The receiving rule is to "meet the pass," which means going *into* the pass instead of waiting in a stationary position for the pass. When defended, it is necessary to move toward the ball until contact is made to ensure possession.

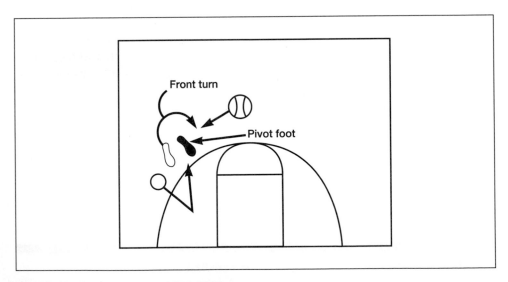

FIGURE 5-13 Catch and face.

PRACTICE

All drills that involve dribbling, passing, and catching are ballhandling drills.

SUMMARY:

- Ballhandling is described as dribbling and passing-catching.
- Dribbling skills should be developed according to the following rules: dribbling is a touch skill; keep your head and face up; use the push-pull motion; dribble legally and with a purpose; learn to use either hand; and, when you are closely guarded, protect the ball.
- Dribble moves that can be used in games include: control or low dribble; speed or high dribble; change-of-pace move; crossover or switch dribble; spin dribble; back dribble and behind-the-back dribble; and, between-the-legs dribble.
- Passing and catching skills are essential to breaking down a team defense and the primary weapon of offense.
- The basic principles of passing include: quickness, target, and timing; pass first, dribble last, shoot when you are open; pass to the open player, the passer and catcher are both responsible for the pass; air passes are the quickest, which include the lob pass and the bounce pass; and, play two-handed basketball.
- Chest air, chest bounce, overhead, baseball, and one-hand push are the basic passes that players should develop.
- Basic catching principles include: be ready, with both hands up; see the ball and catch the ball with your feet in the air, using a jump stop; catch and face/chin, play two-handed basketball, catching the ball with your eyes; and give a target.

Assessment 5-1

Name _____   Section _____   Date _____

Description:

Pairs of players with a ball and a basket area—one passer and one receiver. The receiver gets open with proper spacing, receives the pass with feet in the air, catches the ball, quick stops, and faces in a triple threat position. The passer then becomes the next receiver. The drill involves continuous passing and catching. All passing-catching rules are followed (see Figure 5-14).

Progression:

Perform this drill twice weekly for five minutes. The variations used are (1) passing only, (2) dribble drive with passing, and (3) backdoor moves after pass fakes. A designated pass or pass fake may also be used.

Learning Points:

Get open with a V cut at the right time; catch the ball with feet in the air; catch and face; pass and move at the right time; stay in a stance with the ball in TT; if you do not have the ball, have your hands ready; watch spacing (stay 15–18 feet apart); and, play two-handed basketball.

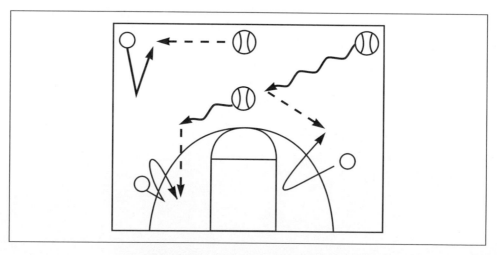

FIGURE 5-14 Drill—moving pairs passing.

47

Assessment 5-2

Name   Section   Date

Description:

Start on one baseline and perform dribble moves in circuits (down and back). Maintain eye contact on the opposite basket: speed dribble–down the court with one hand and return with the other hand; change-of-pace dribble—alternate speed and control dribbles down the court (use opposite hand on return); crossover dribble—with offensive zigzag moves; spin dribble—with offensive zigzag; dribble rocker at the free throw lines and half line; behind-the-back dribble (preferred to non-preferred hand); between-the-legs dribble.

Progression:

Simulate all dribble moves without the ball one circuit, then repeat the circuit with the ball. A behind-the-back progression in the standing position should be used. The between-the-legs dribble should first be practiced with walking steps.

Learning Points:

Do it properly, then do it quickly; work up to "game moves at game speed"; all dribbling principles need to be emphasized, select one point of emphasis to concentrate on each day.

Assessment 5-3

Name   Section   Date

Description:

All basic passes can be practiced against the wall. A target may also be added. The tossback, a commercial passing rebound device, is especially helpful for practicing this skill. It rewards a good pass and informs the athlete when an inaccurate pass is made. The following passes should be used: chest air, chest bounce, overhead, baseball, and push—left hand and right hand.

Progression:

Start with ten passes of each type done twice weekly; use timed passing—catching for thirty seconds with each type pass. Record the number of pass-catch completions.

Learning Points:

Review one point of emphasis daily; full extension and pronation of arms.

Assessment 5-4

Name   Section   Date

Description:

Use the two-hand underhand ball toss (with backspin) to any spot desired on the floor. Make a V cut to get open at that spot and catch the ball. Catch and face the basket; repeat.

Progression:

Twenty-five repetitions in varied locations done twice weekly.

Learning Points:

Put the ball at a target; make a V cut before getting open; catch the ball in the air after one bounce; catch and face the basket in basketball position.

CHAPTER 6

BASICS OF
SHOOTING

OBJECTIVES

After reading this chapter, you should be able to:

- Shoot the ball correctly.
- Understand the proper technique of free throw shooting.

KEY TERMS

While reading this chapter, you will become familiar with the following terms:

▶ **Angle of Release**

▶ **BEEF Principle**

▶ **Follow Through**

   Shooting is probably the best known fundamental skill—every basketball player is interested in scoring. A player's first exposure to a basket and goal will invariably result in dribbling and shooting.

   Historically, shooting has improved over the years. Since the advent of the last new individual shooting skill—the jump shot—in the 1940s, there has been a steady yearly increase in field goal shooting percentages. Today, the national average for college men's basketball is almost 50 percent for two point field goals and over 35 percent for three-point field goals.

Shooting is a skill that can be practiced alone and it produces immediate feedback. It is the fundamental that players enjoy and practice most. Everyone can become a good shooter because good shooters are made through long hours, days, and eventually years of practice.

This chapter examines two primary areas of shooting: field goals, layins, set shot, jump shot, post shot, and free throws.

FIELD GOAL SHOOTING

Develop your Knowledge, Attitude, and Practice habit (KAP) to become a scorer, not only a shooter. Anyone can shoot, but skill is required to score. Here is the KAP principle to remember:

(K) *Knowledge* must be gained about shooting. If you are a beginner, then adopt a complete method; if you are experienced, then always *listen* to new ideas and adapt those that can bring improvement. Be receptive to advice. The measure of shooting success is your shooting percentage. Shooting percentages usually tell the true story.

(A) Develop a proper shooting *attitude*. This consists of: *concentrating* on each shot attempt. Focus on the target and visualize the perfect shot every time. Ignore distractions and see the "net" in your mind. You will develop *confidence* over time. This can be aided by a player developing self respect. Provide self-feedback on each shot. Made shots are remembered and reinforced, while missed shots are analyzed and forgotten. For example, "great shot" on a made basket, or "off balance to the left" on a missed shot might be appropriate self-talk. You should never "beat yourself up" for a missed shot. It is more productive to evaluate the error and then forget it. Get back in the game mentally.

(P) *Practice* can make a shooter into a scorer. This is the secret of good shooting. Physically practice by spending regular quality time shooting. You must learn to practice game shots at game spots at game speed. Visualizing shooting situations and specific shots can also serve as excellent practice. Use your emotions and senses to paint a vivid and complete picture.

Get the shot first by moving to get open. Passing and jump stops are the most important shooting fundamentals. Catch and face in the triple threat (TT) position and be ready to shoot. Triple threat means you can shoot, pass, or dribble quickly from this position. The ball position is sometimes called "the shooting pocket" where the ball is placed near the strong-side armpit. Figure 6-1 shows the offensive player who "pits" the ball.

Attack the basket whenever possible by getting shots as close to the basket as possible on a dribble drive to the basket. Challenge the defense by probing for the basket. The ultimate shot is the lay-up.

FIGURE 6-1A Triple-threat position–front view.

FIGURE 6-1B Triple-threat position–side view.

Performance Tip

The BEEF Principle:

(B) *Balance*. The shot starts from the foundation of proper footwork and the body balanced in ready position. The head goes straight up and down or toward the basket—never laterally.

(E) *Elbow*. The shooting elbow should be up, in, and under the ball (Figure 6-2).

(E) *Eyes*. The shooter should pick up and see the target early. Use narrow concentration to focus on the back of the rim, directly into the basket, (for a rim shot) or on the upper corner of the rectangle (when at a 45° angle to the backboard and banking the ball).

(F) *Follow through*. The shooting arm is completely extended at the elbow and flexed at the wrist. Know the look and the feel of a perfect shot by practicing game shots at game spots at game speed. Do it properly, then quickly. Every shot is a pass (to the basket) and every pass is a shot. Be quick, on target, at the right time, and use fakes. The medium arc shot (about 60° at the **angle of release**) is the best compromise between the best arc for shooting and the available strength for accurate shooting. The shooting foot, elbow, wrist, and hand are in the same plane with the basket as the ball is brought up past the face. Your hand and arm motion is the same on set or jump shots—power comes from the legs. Backspin on the ball produced by finger thrust/wrist snap allows the ball to increase the angle of rebound from the rim (i.e., bounce more vertically and have a greater chance to go in). This action produces a "soft" shot.

SHOOTING TECHNIQUE

A good shot starts from the floor up. Your feet should be ready with the dominant foot slightly forward and your body in ready position facing the basket in triple threat.

To grip use the following steps:

Step 1—The fingers on your shooting hand should be spread comfortably with the ball touching the whole hand, except the heel of your hand. This position can be found by placing the ball on your shooting hand while holding your palm up in front of your body (Figure 6-3a).

Step 2—Your wrist should be locked and cocked—lock your wrist in and cock it back (see two wrinkles) (Figure 6-3b).

Step 3—Keep the elbow up, in, and in front of your wrist (Figure 6-3c). Beginners may have a lower starting elbow position, but their elbow should still be ahead of their wrist. The ball is *in the shooting pocket* and controlled by your balance hand.

The target is the backboard. For a bank shot use the upper corner of the rectangle on the same side as the shot is taken. This target should be used on most shots close to the basket as well as shots "on the angle" (45° to the backboard, see Figure 6-4).

FIGURE 6-2 Hold the ball in shooting position—balance hand on the side.

FIGURE 6-3A Learn to shoot—one hand with no target.

▶ **BEEF Principle**

A shooter should remember balance, elbow, eyes, and follow through are the key factors to successful scoring.

▶ **Angle of Release**

A medium arc shot has about a 60° angle of release, the best compromise between the best arc for shooting and the available strength for accurate shooting.

When the basket ring is the target, it is recommended that you focus on the middle eyelet on the back of the rim. This shot will still have a chance to be made even if it is short or if a player gets tired. Keep your eyes on the target during the whole shot.

Thrust your fingers up and forward through the ball. Keep them firm but not tight. Visualize shooting out of the top of a glass telephone booth or over a seven-foot defender. If the fingers thrust the ball up and over, with good wrist snap, backspin will be produced on the ball.

FIGURE 6-3B Learn to shoot—lock and cock wrist.

FIGURE 6-3C The shooting elbow should be up, in, and under the ball.

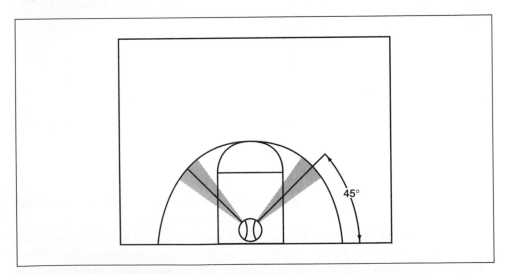

FIGURE 6-4 Angle shots—use the backboard.

Follow through with complete elbow extension, arm pronation and wrist flexion firm but be relaxed. Visualize putting your hand in the basket by making a parachute (imagine a floating hand) and hold it for one full count.

LAY-UPS

All players should learn to shoot both left-and right-handed lay-ups. Jump off your left leg when shooting right-handed and vice versa when shooting left-handed. High jump by "stamping" on the last step (minimize the forward long jump). Use the backboard whenever possible except on the baseline dribble drive and the dunk shot. The dunk shot should be used when a player can dunk the ball without strain and there is minimal defensive traffic. Attack the basket by accelerating to the "hole." Take the ball up with two hands (bring your free hand to the ball when dribbling) and keep it on the side away from the defender and pit the ball (Figure 6-5a). Time the last dribble with the step on your inside foot when using a dribble drive move (Figure 6-5b). Snap your knee up high when jumping and straighten just before the peak of the jump. Shoot softly with a feather touch, focus on the ball and the target (Figure 6-5c).

FIGURE 6-5A Lay-up basics—two-hand pickup.

FIGURE 6-5B Lay-up basics—ball to shoulder.

▶ **Follow Through**

When shooting the basketball the elbow should be extended, arm pronated, and the wrist flexed but relaxed.

TYPES OF LAY-UPS

The overhand or push lay-up (palm facing backboard) is normally used (Figure 6-6a). The underhand or scoop lay-up (palm up) produces a softer shot. The *reach-back,* is used on a baseline drive when going under the basket (Figure 6-6b). The right hand is used when driving from the right and the left hand is used when driving from the right. The ball is shot directly in front of and above the head. Your back will be to the basket in this instance. The *power lay-up,* is used in defensive traffic where body control is more important than timing (Figure 6-6c). It is a slower stronger shot. A jump stop is made with your feet and trunk parallel to the baseline, using a two-foot, two-handed shot. Your outside hand is used to power the ball to the backboard, while using your body for protection.

SET JUMP SHOTS

The *one hand set shot* and *jump shot* are the same except the jump shot is executed by using the set shot just before the peak of a jump. The jump shot is a variation of the set shot. The ball is released just before the peak of the jump on a jump shot.

Stationary spot shots from a pass situation occur when the player can throw a spin pass out in front, retrieve it with a jump stop, and shoot a spot shot (Figure 6-7).

FIGURE 6-5C Lay-up basics—hand behind ball.

FIGURE 6-6A Overhand or push lay-up.

FIGURE 6-6B Reachback lay-up.

FIGURE 6-6C Power lay-up.

FIGURE 6-7A Spot shots.

When moving spot shots from a pass situation, the jump stop with a jump from the basket side foot is recommended (some coaches prefer the plant and pivot technique with the plant made on the basket side foot). These shots can be practiced by using the spin pass to yourself or with the aid of a passing partner.

FIGURE 6-7B Spot shots.

Another type of shot is the *moving spot shot from a dribble situation.* The same footwork is used for this situation as for the pass situation. However, your footwork must be coordinated with the dribble. The last dribble is coordinated with the last step on the basket or your inside foot. On the plant and pivot technique, the last dribble is timed with the plant step. The last dribble is a "hard" dribble to seat the ball in the whole hand and allow it to be moved quickly to the shooting pocket. Your inside shoulder should also be lowered as your body is turned into the "facing" shooting position. This makes it difficult for the defender to tell whether the shooter is driving to the basket or pulling up to shoot.

For a three-point shot use proper set shot technique, and be sure you are balanced. The plant and pivot footwork requires more leg power. Be sure you are open when you take more time to shoot this longer shot.

POST-HOOK SHOTS

The post-hook shot is a modified lay-up used by players who receive the ball in a low-post position with their back to the basket. This location is just outside the free throw lane near the "block" on or near the post line as seen in Figure 6-8 (straight line from ball to basket). Catch the ball in the low-post area with the ball in a "chinit" position. A rear turn pivot is made into the lane using the baseline foot as the pivot foot. The other foot is used to step into the lane as far as possible in the balanced position. Ideally, this foot is parallel to the baseline. When the non-pivot foot hits the floor, the pivot foot is raised as the knee is lifted high and rotated as in a normal layin. The ball is moved from the chinning position past the

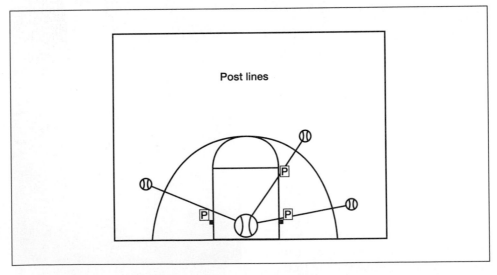

FIGURE 6-8 Posting up "on the block".

side of the head, pushed overhead, and released with full arm extension and pronation. The move is led by the inside elbow.

The complete post shot sequence as illustrated in figure 6-9 includes: chinit (chin the ball for protection); rear turn and step across; move the ball up and over with full extension and pronation (keep the ball close to your body); rotate and shoot the post shot; land in ready position with the assumption the shot will be missed. Be ready to rebound if it is missed.

FIGURE 6-9A The post shot—post up.

FIGURE 6-9B The post shot—catch and chin the ball.

FIGURE 6-9C The post shot—shoot and follow through.

FREE THROW SHOOTING

Free throw shooting percentages in basketball remain relatively constant for the past thirty years. This has occurred even though field goal shooting has improved steadily for over forty years.

Your free throw shooting should improve if you do the following: practice in proportion to the scoring importance in a game (approximately 20 percent) and practice free throw shooting whenever you play. Develop your free throw shooting (know the proper techniques, develop a good shooting attitude, and practice regularly) every time you play.

BASIC TECHNIQUES

Align on the dot. The shooting foot, elbow, hand, and ball are aligned in a plane with the basket. The alignment of the shooting foot should be in the same spot every time and about 10° to the left. The balance foot is about 45° to the left. (See Figure 6-10.)

Grip the ball on the whole shooting hand. The balance hand should be on the side or under the ball. The shooting index finger should be on the air hole. The wrist is locked in and cocked back. The elbow is up, in, and in front of the wrist. Keep the ball in.

You should be in modified ready position with weight over the front foot and head steady. Start and finish with weight forward. Focus on the center eyelet on the back of the rim or shoot above and over the center of the front of the rim. Figure 6-11a illustrates the starting position. See and say "net" in your mind. At the

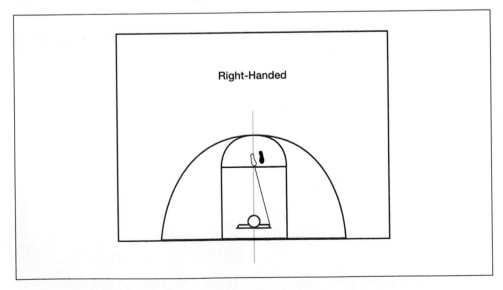

FIGURE 6-10 Free throw foot alignment.

FIGURE 6-11A The free throw starting position.

FIGURE 6-11B The free throw ending position.

bottom of the shot, use all positive motion to the basket. *Follow through* with full extension and pronation. Using leg power, come up off the floor. Hold your follow through until the ball goes through the net (Figure 6-11b).

Developing a ritual is an important part of successful free throw shooting. It is much easier to groove a pattern that is always the same. To relax, take a deep breath before you shoot.

SUMMARY

- Field goal shooting principles were explained as: shooting basics, *develop knowledge, improve shooting attitude,* and *practice* (both mental and physical); *attack the basket,* challenge the defense; and follow the *BEEF principle.*
- Field goal shooting techniques were focused on: *balance, hands ready, wrist, elbow, ball, target, shoot up and over,* and *follow through.*
- Lay-up shots should be learned according to the following rules: use both right and left hands; high jump off the opposite leg; use the backboard unless shooting a dunk shot; attack the basket; take the ball up with two hands and protect it on the outside; time the last dribble with the step of the inside foot; bring outside knee high when jumping and snap knee straight just before the peak of jump; shoot softly against the backboard; focus on the ball and the target.

- The types of lay-up shots that should be learned: include overhand and underhand, reachback, and power.
- Set shot and jump shot rules are similar. The jump shot is a variation of the set shot.
- Stationary spot shots from a pass, moving spot shots from a pass, and moving spot shots from a dribble are shot variations.
- Post or hook shots are used by low-post players with their back to the basket.
- Basic free throw shooting techniques center on following a ritual.

Assessment 6-1

Name   Section   Date

Progression:

Two lines in the lane—shoot using the backboard first, then close shots to targets (rim and backboard); without the ball develop footwork as a lead in progression. Spin pass the basketball to yourself. Each shooter takes a shot and rebounds until it is made. The next shooter gets open while calling passer's name. After the name is called, the passer makes a pass to the shooter and goes to the end of the opposite line. Continue and repeat. From a dribble, the shooter rebounds his or her own shot made, passes back to the next person in line, and goes to end of the opposite line.

Learning Points:

Use "V" cuts to get open; get the shot and hit the shot. Tell the passer you are open by calling his/her name. Pass only when your name is called. To be ready for a rebound—assume the shot will be missed. Shoot from all locations on the floor.

Assessment 6-2

Name   Section   Date

Description:

This is a continuous shooting drill that incorporates all principles of movement, passing/catching, shooting, and offensive rebounding. Players are grouped in pairs (there may be one or two pairs per basket). With a rebounder under the basket with a ball, a teammate gets open for a shot. Call out the rebounder's name and he or she receives pass for shot. The shooter rebounds the shot until a basket is made (assume the shot will be missed), then gains possession for pass to a teammate who has moved outside for a shot. The receiver must always get open and call the passer's name. The passer makes a pass to a teammate for a good shot and goes quickly to another location near the edge of the power zone. Be ready to move only when a teammate has scored and has ball possession.

Each player gets open and shoots while a teammate stays as rebounder. Alternate shooter after thirty seconds. Make five baskets and switch. Another variation is a game to ten made baskets. Moving with shots from a pass; you must go somewhere on the V cut. Designate a type of pass and type of shot (regular, jab fake and shot.) Apply some type of false pressure on the shooter such as shouting, a hand in face or contact. The defender cannot block the shot or foul the shooter. At least once a week use the variation of defender with "hands up" for the shooter to improve arch. Consider three pass shooting by using an outlet pass (passer posts up), pass to post (passer cuts), and return pass for shot.

Another variation is one shooter competes against a designated "star" shooter with a partner designated as rebounder. The game is begun with a free throw and is completed with shooting set or jump shots. The scoring rules are as follows: the free throw (+1 for shooter on make, -3 for star on miss), field goal (+1 for shooter on make, -2 for star on miss). The game can be played to eleven or twenty-one points.

Progression:

Ten minutes of two variations daily. Gradually introduce and increase competitive shooting. Practice shooting in all game situations.

Assessment 6-3

Name   Section   Date

Description:

Free throw practice should include physical and mental practice. It should follow the sequence of shooting consecutive shots. Shoot twenty free throws before each class or practice session and keep records of the successful shots. It is also helpful for you to attempt and make a maximum number of consecutive free throws in a practice situation. For example, the "5" club or the "10" club. Mentally practice while waiting to shoot free throws on the court and for any five-minute period off the court. Paint vivid pictures and practice perfect performance.

Shoot in competitive situations (i.e., "row" free throws—a given number of made free throws in a row). For example, make three in a row. A variation of this game is called team free throws. A group of players is divided into a team of six to eight players at the two main baskets on a court. They remain at that basket until each player, in order, makes a free throw consecutively. At that time the teams switch baskets and repeat the process. Number of "row" free throws a group of two, three, or four players can make in a designated period. A five-minute period is ideal for this variation.

Net shots, is another shooting game to a designated number or for a designated time. Count 1 for a net shot, -1 for rim hit, and -2 for a miss. Also try shooting free throws in pairs with your eyes closed. This is done once a week for a five-minute period. Your partner provides exact information on shot location. Shots are usually taken in sets of three.

Assessment 6-4

Name   Section   Date

Description:

This package of shooting drills is recommended whenever practicing to become a complete shooter. It is a self-teaching program designed to help each player develop from a shooter into a scorer. This is truly the secret to good shooting: K—know how to shoot; A—develop a shooting attitude; P—practice (physical and mental).

Foundation Fifty Program

- Ten free throws
- Four foundation shots:
  * Two form shots—perfect shots taken overhead, against a wall, or against the backboard without shooting at a target.
  * Three mind shots - paint vivid pictures of two specific game shots (free throw or field goal) in key situations. Practice perfect shots and shut out all errors from the mind.
  * Five close shot game shots—taken in the free throw lane 6–10 feet from the basket in all possible locations, including the 45° angle backboard shot.
  * Ten choice shots—practice a favorite shot.
  * Ten shots from a spin pass—*stationary* spot shots in the locations, positions, and range that each player will use against all types of defenses.
  * Ten shots from a spin pass to self—moving left (five) and moving right (five).
  * Ten shots taken off the dribble, (five) to the right and (five) to the left.

Learning Points:

Shoot game shots from game spots at game speed. Visualize the defenders on each shot as well as "quality" mental practice to develop your confidence. Know what a good shot looks like and what a good shot feels like. Teach yourself to shoot each time you practice.

Assessment 6-5

Name   Section   Date

Progression:
Make five shots of each type.
- **Form shots**—see and feel one hand shots with no target.
- **Close shots**—always start in close to the basket (use both the backboard and rim as a target).
- **Stationary shots**—use a spin pass to shoot from your favorite spot.
- **Shots from a pass**—use a spin pass. Take five reps doing footwork only (no shot) and then five regular made shots.
- **Shots from a dribble**—five reps without shooting and five reps shooting.

Assessment 6-6

_____ _____ _____
Name   Section   Date

Description:

All tasks in this drill are self-testing. They require you to meet *effective* standards of scoring. All moves are to be carried out consecutively without rest—game shots at game spots at game speeds.

Dribble drive layin moves—from left and right corners (with foot on sideline) and at each hash mark at sideline and at the top of the key. Only one dribble is allowed and one basket must be made from each spot. The object is to cover the greatest distance possible with a "lay-up" scoring move. After each basket is made, you earn the right to take a free throw. The free throw must be made or you repeat the field goal move.

Jump-set shots—taken from five spots with spin pass moves and dribble moves to left and right. The same field goal shooting objectives must be met, (i.e., two in a row at each spot). This is immediately followed by a free throw. The free throw is made or the field goal move is repeated.

Make it-Take it Row Shooting Practice Tips:

• *Dribble Drive*—left corner/free throw; left hash marks/free throw; top of key/free throw; right hash mark/free throw; right corner/free throw.

• *Spin pass field goals*—game shots/game spots/game speed; field goals/free throw.

• *Field goals from the dribble*—game shots/game spots/game speed.

  Note: Inside players should substitute inside moves for shots from the dribble.

77

CHAPTER 7

REBOUNDING—
A KEY SKILL

▼

OBJECTIVES

After reading this chapter, you should be able to:

*   Understand the importance of rebounding.
*   Perform defensive rebounding.
*   Perform offensive rebounding.

KEY TERMS

While reading this chapter, you will become familiar with the following terms:

► **Assume Principle**

► **Blockout**

► **Chinit**

► **Garbage Rebounder**

► **Overhead Rebound and Shot**

Rebounding is a fundamental skill that depends more on discipline, aggressiveness, and determination than on the overemphasized jumping ability and height.

The importance of rebounding lies in its value. It has been estimated that 80 percent of possessions come from defensive rebounding and made baskets (about equally divided) with the remaining possessions coming from opponent's errors, steals, and offensive rebounds (repossessions). Thus, rebounding is the most important method of gaining ball possession for a team.

Research findings indicate that teams who are national leaders in rebounding win a higher percentage of their games than national free throw or field goal percentage leaders. One study over a ten-year period found that in games won, the opponents were out rebounded 80 percent of the time (and vice versa).

Defensive rebounding (i.e., the ability to allow the opponent only one contests shot) is one of the most important aspects of defense. One of the essential elements of a fast break is the beginning, commonly started by a defensive rebound.

An offensive rebound is a "second life" for the offense because it is a repossession of something lost. Individually, an effective rebounder is often highly respected by teammates because rebounding is usually underpublicized.

The most important principle in rebounding is to **assume** every shot will be missed and rebound *every* shot *every* time.

Rebound distribution favors certain floor areas. When a shot is taken from the side, 70–75 percent of the rebounds will go opposite (helpside) with the middle being the next frequented area. Whenever possible, especially where contact is expected, rebounding should be done from two feet with two hands.

Performance Tip

The Assume Principle

To become a good overall rebounder, assume *every shot* will be missed. Always go to the offensive boards and make contact *every time* on defensive rebounding.

▶ **Assume Principle**
Rebound every shot every time.

DEFENSIVE REBOUNDING

There are several different theories regarding the best techniques to use in defensive rebounding: turn and go to the boards; rebound from zone areas; and blockout each opponent and rebound.

This book's principles of defensive rebounding are based on the latter theory. This theory is developed from the assumption that it will be effective with talent that is equal or inferior to that of the opponent.

The skills of defensive rebounding are to: see the ball; assume a miss; pressure every shot; see the player, go to the player, blockout; go to the ball, capture the ball, keep the ball, and outlet the ball.

BASIC PRINCIPLES

See the ball—the first rebounding rule is to be alert for a shot that may produce a rebound. *Assume,* because the most important rule of rebounding is to create a positive attitude toward the skill. This is done by thinking and acting as if every shot will produce a rebound (i.e., assume every shot will be missed).

Pressure every shot because when you are guarding the shooter you are responsible for applying defensive pressure. This consists of voice (shot call) and physical pressure. Be close with a hand in the face (wrist back) to alter the shot. Stay in your stance and don't leave the floor until the shooter does (see Figure 7-1). *Seeing the player* is one of the few times when you must avoid watching the ball. When the ball is in the air, it is necessary to look for and locate your assigned offensive player.

Go to the assigned player to take away a player's momentum. Always blockout the shooter. For the nonshooter there are two situations you will face: (1) if an offensive player has moved into a you-ball-basket position close to the basket it is important to fight around instantly and (2) if you are unsuccessful, try to make body contact with your hands up, and *tip* the ball outaway from the backboard if the rebound cannot be gained with two hands. Inside the three-point line, blockout by going to the offensive player's location to make contact (Figure 7-2). Outside the three-point line, visually locate the offensive player then turn and go to the ball. **NOTE:** Closeout is critical on the helpside and when guarding a good rebounder. It has been estimated that 70–75 percent of rebounds occur on the helpside.

FIGURE 7-1 Stay in your stance— pressure shot.

Blockout shooters everywhere and nonshooters inside the power zone.

The recommended technique is to go to the offensive player and give a path then take it away. Only give the offensive player one choice. When close to the player, swing a foot across with a front turn (match the defender's left foot to the offensive player's left foot or right to right) (Figure 7-3a). Follow quickly with a rear turn to make contact with the opponent (Figures 7-3b and c). Use *bumpers* to make and keep contact (front turn, rear turn, make contact). Keep your feet active in BP. Your elbows are out and your arms are straight up in an elbow-to-elbow *blockout* surface (Figure 7-4).

Assume BP for rebounding with hands up, and elbows out. Be big, make contact, and move to the ball. Remember to keep your eyes on the ball. *Capture the ball* by taking charge of the ball with two hands at the peak of the jump. The ball may be blocked with one hand if it is brought to the other hand immediately. Tip the ball *only* if it is to prevent the offense from gaining possession. Land in a "spread eagle" BP with ball located on your forehead for a quick outlet pass or under your chin if you are in traffic or congestion (chinit).

FIGURE 7-2 Defensive blockout when the opponent is inside.

FIGURE 7-3A Blockout—front turn.

▶ **Blockout**

Locate an opponent after a shot is put up and be in the "you-ball-basket" position.

FIGURE 7-3B Blockout—rear turn.

FIGURE 7-3C Blockout—contact.

FIGURE 7-4 Blockout—arms up, elbows out.

This is called chinning the ball and is one of the most secure methods of protecting the ball in congestion anywhere on the floor. To chin the ball, you should assume a BP, keep your elbows out, your head up, and your fingers spread and pointing up to squeeze the ball firmly. Don't dangle the ball, **chinit** (see Figure 7-5). **NOTE:** Use the "roll and fold" technique under extremely heavy pressure or for a last possession (Figure 7-6).

Get the ball out by using an air pass up the floor. Use pivots to face the sideline to make the easiest available pass. Open your body away from the opponent and pass the ball quickly. The dribble outlet should be used if no pass outlets are open up the floor. When this happens, use the "step through" move directly up the floor to open the passing lanes.

FIGURE 7-5A Chinit—rebound the ball.

FIGURE 7-5B Chinit—open court protection.

The mental aspects of rebounding are even more significant than the actual rebounding skills. You should develop speed, quickness and strength. Use your physical qualities to their utmost and then learn to conserve time and space. You will also need to learn to anticipate by seeing the ball and know when and where each shot is taken. Remember, short shots tend to rebound short and long three-point shots tend to rebound long. Know rebound areas on a shot from the side; the priority areas are helpside, middle, and ballside. Shots from the middle usually rebound in the middle.

The rebound characteristics of each ball, backboard, and rim may be slightly different; examine each situation and become aware of it.

FIGURE 7-6 Roll and fold rebound.

▶ **Chinit**
The most secure method of protecting the ball in congestion anywhere on the basketball court.

OFFENSIVE REBOUNDING

The *Assume* principle, that every shot will be missed, is also the most important principle of this phase of rebounding. With a low percentage possibility for success, the offensive rebounder must develop the self-discipline to go to the boards each time a shot is taken. Assuming a 50 percent shooting percentage and a 70 percent defensive rebounding percentage, the offensive team will only get 15 rebounds out of every possible 100. Each player's equal share would then be only three (one-fifth) out of 100 possible rebounds. This assumes that there are no substitutes.

Therefore, it can readily be seen that the good offensive rebounder must be aggressive, determined, and disciplined. When the odds are against you, then you must be prepared to meet those few opportunities for success.

BASIC PRINCIPLES

Become a **garbage rebounder.** This is a term for a completely reliable player. Develop a "nose for the ball," a sixth sense for rebounding. Want the ball and find a way to get it.

Practice offensive rebounding at all practices in drill situations when a shot is taken. It should be treated as game competition. Stay after the ball until it is in the basket or the defense gains possession.

Meet the objectives of offensive rebounding. Make contact by blocking out or blocking in. The ideal position results in the offensive rebounder gaining the inside position to *blockout* the defender. The offensive player can also *blockin* the defender that gets too far under the basket.

Avoiding contact is a secondary objective when the defender has the advantage. The offensive rebounder has an equal chance to get the rebound when even with the defender and a greater chance when ahead of the defender. Never be satisfied with being blocked out or just lean on the defender.

Pressure the defensive rebounder. If the offensive player doesn't get the rebound and the opponent does, the rebounder should be contained and harassed immediately. Prevent the quick outlet pass or dribble.

Performance Tip

Offensive Rebounds

Always go to rebound on every shot.

Use quick moves that avoid contact and put the offensive rebounder at a disadvantage. From BP use a quick step past the defender. A zigzag move can be used to fake one way and step past pressure on the defender's back. A pivot may be used to block out or get even. Have your hands up anytime you are in the rebounding area. This allows you to be ready for the quick rebound and for quick jumps.

Develop scoring moves to be used when you secure possession and are open. Tipping is a controlled shot. This is only recommended when two hands are used and the ball is controlled. The ball may be tipped out to yourself or to a teammate with one hand if there is no other alternative. Your arms should be fully extended overhead and your elbows locked. Tip with your wrists and fingers.

The ball is secured with a quick jump and is kept directly **overhead.** You land in BP and make an immediate power move to the basket. This move is used before the defender is set and is in position.

The power move is used in "traffic" to ensure possession and when there is a strong chance to score if contacted or fouled. Capture the ball, chinit, and explode to the backboard (Figure 7-7). Use a shot fake with the ball before a power or explosion move. This is designed for

you to get the defender to leave his/her feet, get out of BP, and draw the foul. The rebounder captures the ball, chins it, lifts, and then explodes to the basket. Keep contact on the basket and see the defender with peripheral vision. Assume the chinit position, fake with the head, and stay in BP with legs locked. Repeated fakes may be necessary (Figure 7-8).

It is necessary to protect the ball. Chinning it will prevent the slap up from smaller players trying to dislodge the ball from your hands. Good rebounders avoid "tie ups" by having a "hands up" position. Inside scoring moves should be "to the glass" (i.e., using the backboard whenever possible). The exception to this rule would be a dunk shot.

FIGURE 7-7 Power move to score.

▶ **Garbage Rebounder**
The term for a player who is completely reliable when it comes to a rebounding position.

▶ **Overhead Rebound and Shot**
The ball is secured with a quick jump and is kept directly overhead.

FIGURE 7-8A Chinit.

FIGURE 7-8B Fake.

FIGURE 7-8C Score.

SUMMARY

- Height and jumping ability are great assets in rebounding, yet the factors of discipline and determination are more important.
- Offensively, rebounding is the backbone of the fast break, as well as a "second life" for the offense.
- Assume that every shot will be missed then you will be ready for rebounding.
- Blocking out is every player's responsibility when rebounding.
- Chinit is a ball protection technique useful in rebounding any time there is congestion or whenever ball control is challenged by the defense.
- The basic rules for offensive rebounding are to anticipate shots, become a garbage player, blockout-blockin, keep hands up, and score or pass out when getting a rebound.
- Use the backboard whenever possible.

Assessment 7-1

Name   Section   Date

Description:

    Defensive boards—The first player in each line sprints on the court at 6–15 feet from the basket in defensive BP. The teacher/coach designates ball location (left or right). On the command "rebound," each player simulates the blockout, captures the rebound, chins the ball, and makes an outlet pass. Then the next four players sprint onto the floor in BP.

    Boards in pairs—The first four players sprint onto the floor in an offensive BP (one in TT—left or right) near the power zone, and the next four assume a proper defensive BP to pressure that ball and support the ball defender. On the command "shot," all four defenders carry out defensive rebound assignments. All must make contact.

Learning Points:

    Call *shot* and make contact. Keep your hands above your shoulders, with elbows out. Chinit with your fingers up and your elbows out. Pivot and outlet the ball.

Assessment 7-2

Name _____ Section _____ Date _____

Description:
   This is a defensive rebounding and passing drill. When receiving any pass, call the passer's name while getting open. The first player X_1, passes to X_4, gets open for a return pass received with a quick stop in the free throw lane, and tosses the ball underhand above the rectangle level to simulate a defensive rebound.
   X_1 angle jumps to the ball, captures the ball with two hands, puts the ball on the forehead, makes a front turn on the right pivot foot, and outlet passes to X_4. X_4 passes to X_2 and then goes to the back of the line.
Learning Points:
   Pass receivers get open and call passer's name; receive every pass with a quick stop. Toss the ball above the rectangle level on the backboard with a two-hand underhand toss. Angle jump to the ball and capture it with two hands, ball to forehead, front turn and outlet pass. Make every pass quick and accurate (away from the imaginary defender).

Assessment 7-3

Three-on-Three Closeout and Blockout

Name _____   Section _____   Date _____

Description:

The drill is played as a competitive three-on-three "make it, take it" drill that only is restarted when a basket is made. On the defensive rebound situation, the defense must outlet the ball above the "top of key" area before going on offense. The teacher/coach may require the defending three to stay on defense whenever an assignment is missed.

Progression:

Three lines underneath the basket—offensive, defensive boards; six players at each basket.

Learning Points:

See the player, call shot; make contact with the hands above the shoulders; capture the ball with two hands, chinit; front turn and outlet the ball to a teammate above the free throw line extended.

Progression:

Six defensive rebound and outlets, first with the ball on right side, then on the left side.

Assessment 7-4

Name   Section   Date

Description:

The first four players make a "get ahead or even" move from BP, move to the free throw line area, jump quickly, simulate capturing the ball, land in the chinning position, and use a designated scoring move. They repeat this process at the half line, the opposite free throw line, and the opposite baseline. The return is made when all groups of four reach the endline. Offensive spacing (15–18 feet) should be kept with the player immediately ahead.

Progression:

Designate—get ahead or even moves (step through, zigzag, or pivot) and scoring moves (tip, overhead, power, or lift).

Learning Points:

Be quick, but don't hurry. Explode to and capture the ball. Keep your balance by being ready for contact. Take charge of the ball by going, go to the backboard strong. Assume a miss.

Assessment 7-5

Garbage Drill

Name _____   Section _____   Date _____

Description:
There are two lines of players at the free throw line area facing the basket with a ball in each line. The player passes the ball to the backboard with a two-hand underhand toss and rebounds the ball, then uses a designated scoring move. After scoring (stay after it until it's in) the player passes the ball to the next player in line and goes to the end of the opposite line.

Progression:
The sequence used is tips, overheads, power, and fakes (two repetitions on each side). This is followed by live rebounding where both players compete for the ball after a shot by a coach. The player who gains possession is on offense and the other player becomes a defender. Continue until one scores. They may always use the coach as a passing outlet.

Learning Points:
Hands up and assume; rebound with two feet, two hands; use the backboard whenever possible. Take good shots (use scoring moves); use the coach to pass and move to get open score in the "paint" (all shots in free throw lane).

Assessment 7-6

Survival Rebounding

Name   Section   Date

Description:

Groups of four to eight players at each basket with three players in the game at one time. If six to eight players are used, extra players should be shooting free throws until they are rotated into the game. The teacher/coach or assistant is at each basket to shoot the ball (intentional miss) and act as a passing outlet for the rebounder. The rules of competition include: play starts with a missed shot; all three players attempt to get the rebound; the player who obtains the rebound is on offense and the other two players become defenders; rebounders use scoring moves, all shots must be taken in the free throw lane; the rebounder may outlet to the coach and get open for a return pass, there is no boundary for play; three scored baskets by a player allows rotation out (other players retain their totals); severe fouls are the only fouls called. A player may lose a score by fouling or by not playing defense.

Learning Points:

Be aggressive and go to the basket. Use two feet and two hands. Stay after the ball until it's in the basket. Find a way to get the ball and protect the ball—chin it. Pass the ball out if you are not open.

CHAPTER 8

DEFENSE—
ON AND OFF THE BALL

OBJECTIVES

After reading this chapter, you should be able to:

- Understand the importance of defense.
- Know and perform defensive stance and steps on ball and off ball.

KEY TERMS

While reading this chapter, you will become familiar with the following terms:

▶ ATTACK Principle   ▶ Ball-You-Player

▶ Ball-You-Basket

Evidence suggests that winners play good defense, and good defense produces consistent winners. Teams with determination on defense have fewer "off nights" than the team that relies on offense; defense can be more consistent and reliable.

Some coaches believe that losses in basketball games are rooted in defensive break-downs—individual or team defense, defensive rebounding, or turnovers caused by the opponent's defense. Based on this premise, it can be seen that you and your team's defense strongly affect the game outcome. The basics of defense can be used for zone or player-to-player team defense.

An effective team defense is necessary for scoring from the fast break. Aggressive defensive teams often generate fast break scoring opportunities and build offensive confidence as a by-product of capitalizing on their defense.

Individually, defense can do several things. It can build self-confidence. All players can play defense effectively, if they have the determination and are willing to meet the considerable challenges of defense. It can also develop a reputation of aggressiveness and toughness. Finally, it can earn the special pride and self-respect you get from playing at both ends of the court.

NECESSITIES OF DEFENSE

Anticipate the shifts from offense to defense. Organized transition with instant communication among all five players is required. Sprint to defense and then run backward (to see the whole floor) once the offense is contained. Prevent easy scores and gain possession of the ball through rebounds or steals.

Put continuous pressure on the ball. Every shot must be pressured physically and verbally. Constantly bother the "live" player (still with a dribble). Force the dribbler to change direction. Swarm the "dead" player who has used the dribble. All players off the ball should protect the basket and support the point of pressure.

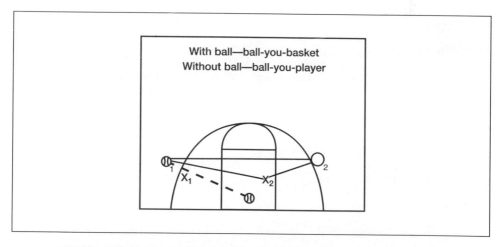

FIGURE 8-1 Defensive positions—ball-you-basket, ball-you-player.

Performance Tip

CONCEPTS OF ATTACK

Pressure defense means action. It is embodied in the word **ATTACK** which provides these basic concepts:

A   for *attitude*—the starting point of all defense is the determination to become an aggressive, intelligent defensive player. You have absolute control of your attitude, especially toward defense.

T   for *teamwork*—the collective efforts of five defensive players are greater than the five individual efforts. Although it is commonly accepted that an individual offensive player will beat an individual defensive player, a good team defense will usually meet most offensive challenges. Good individual defensive players put the team first. Your defensive team must develop the patience to play good defense in all situations regardless of time and score.

T   for *tools of defense*—the basic physical tools are the mind (through your eyes), body, and feet. Play defense with those three and avoid fouling with your hands.

A   for *anticipation*—use basketball sense and judgment triggered by vision. Use your eyes to anticipate; see the ball at all times. For example, a loose ball should be spotted instantly. Possession should be gained with both hands before you make a decision to pass, dribble, or shoot.

C   for *concentration*—be alert and ready to play defense at all times. Know the situation and take away your opponent's strength. Never rest, physically or mentally, on defense.

K   for *keep your stance*—maintain BP at all times. Reduce your gambles, and be ready to take advantage of your opponent's mistakes.

Always maintain basketball position (i.e., stay in stance when on defense). Most fouls occur when you are out of position and not ready. When you are guarding a player with the ball maintain a position of **ball-you-basket.** When you are guarding a player without the ball, maintain the position of **ball-you-player** with the player you are guarding. See the player and the ball. Support ball pressure and protect the basket. See Figure 8-1.

One player always pressures the ball while the four other players play zones to protect the basket and to support the defender on the ball. When on the ball prevent middle of the floor penetration toward the goal with the dribble or with direct air passes to the same area (especially inside the three-point field goal zone).When off the ball keep passes out of the middle of the floor (especially the three-point field goal zone) by defending zones toward the basket area. Play zone and support the ball defender.

Five players should adjust their floor position with every pass. After the ballhandler passes the ball, the defender moves instantly toward the ball and basket, called jumping to the ball. Adjust to the ball-you-player position on every pass and on a dribble move.

Anytime the ball moves past a defender's floor position up the floor, the defender should sprint up the floor through the ballhandler until reaching a point past the ball and then reestablish a defensive stance in a helping position (Figure 8-2). More interceptions are made coming behind the ball than going the other way. Look at the ball and passing lanes as you sprint past the ball.

Each defensive player is responsible for blocking offensive players from the basket area and gaining the defensive rebound when a shot is taken. Players must talk to produce an effective team defense. Essentially, the five players should act as one by talking to teammates.

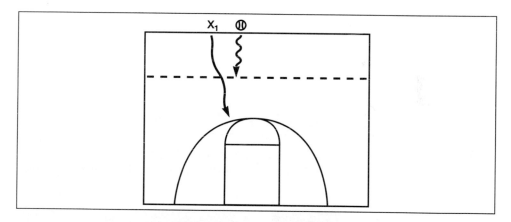

FIGURE 8-2 Ahead of the ball.

▶ **ATTACK Principle**
A mnemonic aid to remember principles of pressure defense: attitude, teamwork, tools of defense, anticipation, concentration, and keep your stance.

▶ **Ball-You-Basket**
A position maintained when a player defends someone with the basketball.

▶ **Ball-You-Player**
A position maintained when a player defends an opponent without the basketball.

DEFENSE ON THE BALL

Pressure on the ball is required at all times. The defensive basketball position (BP) must be learned, assumed, and actively maintained. You assume a proper stance and stay in it with active feet. In addition, your head should always be lower than that of the offensive player with the live ball—your head is even with your opponent's chest. Stay lower than the offensive player.

The basic stance needed is the live ball *(player still with dribble)*—BP with palm up and lead hand (matching front foot) constantly jabbing at the ball (arm flick). You may prefer the lead hand in a palm facing position. The back hand should be up in shoulder area. Closing out on the live ball means sprinting until there is a danger of the offensive player driving by you toward the basket. Break down into BP with both arms up overhead in a "palms facing" position to take away the quick air pass. Approach with the weight back until balance is achieved (Figure 8-3). Prevent penetration of ball or dribbler, then pressure the ball handler. For *dribbler defense* use basic BP, then cut off the path of the dribbler with your body (staying ball-you-basket) by putting your head in front of the ballhandler. Use an arm flick to jab at the ball with your lead hand (when the dribbler is to the defender's right, the defender should use his right arm) (Figure 8-4). If the dribbler gets past the defender, the defender should run to reestablish *ball-you-basket*.

When an offensive player uses a spin, reverse, or whirl dribble, be certain to "get a gap" to avoid being hooked (Figure 8-5). In live ball defense situations stay in your stance, but get both hands around the ball. When in dead ball defense swarm the ball and attack the offensive player's senses (sight, learning, smell, touch). In this instance, you should also stay in your stance.

ON THE BALL PRINCIPLES

Maintain ball-you-basket relationship. You should always be between the ball-handler and the basket to stop the dribbler with your body. Be within touching

FIGURE 8-3 Defender closing out–get in a stance.

FIGURE 8-4 Defending the dribble.

FIGURE 8-5A Defend the spin dribble—turn, head on ball.

FIGURE 8-5B Defend the spin dribble—get a gap.

distance of the ballhandler when the ball is received to invade the offensive player's comfort zone. The inside foot should always be kept up (i.e., keep your belly to the baseline or sideline when near the baseline/sideline) when guarding a ballhandler holding the ball.

Work to prevent dribble penetration and quick air pass penetration by the ballhandler. Move toward the ball and the basket after every pass (i.e., instantly jump to the ball). Reaching for the ball often results in a personal foul. When going for the steal, it is better to go for the ball in the air if good BP can be maintained. In addition, you should always attempt to deflect or steal as many passes as possible.

DEFENSE OFF THE BALL

Defense off the ball is the most challenging and crucial aspect of defense. There is a natural tendency to relax away from the ball. However, this must be prevented at all costs. Remember, basket protection and ball defender support are primary concerns that require your full attention.

The basic stances (BP) away from the ball are open position and closed position. An open position is when the offensive player is in a perimeter position. You are in a ball-you-player relationship with a flat triangle one step off the line of the ball. This is called a "pistols" stance to remind you of the correct position and vision

Performance Tip

Your basic defensive tools are mind/eyes, body, and feet. Defend on-the-ball in a ball-you-basket relationship. Defend off the ball in a ball-you-player relationship.

attained by seeing both the ball and the offensive player, while also pointing fingers at the ball and the offensive player. You should "glance" back and forth if necessary to see the ball and maintain eye contact with the opponent being guarded. The closed position is when the offensive player is in the middle of the defense or farther away from the ball. In the closed stance, you must see the ball and eye contact with the offensive player being guarded must be maintained. In this situation, the defender's lead hand should be in a thumbs down position, with the palm facing the offensive player (Figure 8-6). Stay in your stance.

GENERAL PRINCIPLES

The farther the offensive player is from the ball, the farther you are away from the player being guarded (ball-you-player). Keep a gap. This is also called the "closer the ball is to the defender, the closer the defender should be to the person being guarded" rule. If contact must be made, beat the offensive player to the spot, make contact, and then reestablish the gap.

What you as a defender do before your offensive player gets the ball determines what that player can do with the ball. Initiate a good defensive floor position and stance before the opponent gets the ball to keep the offense out of the middle, and power, zone.

Prevent player cuts to the ball (ball-you-player) in the middle of the defense. Adjust your floor position on every pass. See the ball at all times and use your eyes to anticipate careless passes and offensive player movements. Support pressure on the ball. If there is dribble penetration, the closest defender off the ball should be ready to help and decide. The defender has an option to bluff the dribbler with a defensive fake until the beaten defender reestablishes BP then recovers back to the assigned opponent. This is also called the "fake and threaten" or "hedge" and is useful in all dribble penetration defensive situations (e.g., when defending a two-on-one fast break situation or switching to the penetrating dribbler).

To defend against cutters you should maintain the ball-you-player relationship and work to beat the opponent to the spot in the middle of the defense, or power, zone. Try to avoid contact until the offensive player gets near the middle. Keep a gap and keep in front.

If the offensive player being guarded leaves the side of the front court to open it for a teammate's one-on-one move, you should "open" to the basket area and anticipate a help situation. You should keep vision on the ball. Remember that an offensive player going away from the ball, especially on a "clearout," is usually a decoy or a screener.

FIGURE 8-6 Closed stance—away from the ball.

SPECIAL DEFENSIVE SITUATIONS

For *inside or post defense* keep the ball out of the middle, especially near the free throw lane of the front court. Stay in a ball-you-player position whenever possible by using a closed stance with hand across. When the ball is above the free throw line, you should be above the opponent and when the ball is below, you are below the opponent. Avoid contact whenever possible by keeping a gap. Contact should only be made to hold a desired position briefly. Offensive post players control defenders by establishing and maintaining contact. Keep moving and keep the offensive post player (and passer) guessing. Get in and stay in BP with both hands up and ready. Blockout on every shot and when the offensive post player gets the ball in the low post area, take a step back to gain space and reaction time. Stay in BP.

Avoid defensive screens whenever possible. Screens may be defended against by fighting through. The screened defender may be helped with a "show and go" or "hedge" move by the helping defender (Figure 8-7). Switching is another way a defender cannot get through the screen. It is important to switch up and call the switch. This is done by the player seeing and guarding the screener (Figure 8-8). When switching up, the ballhandler should be contained.

SUMMARY:

- Pressure defense means: A—attitude, T—teamwork, T—tools, A—anticipation, C—concentration, K—keep and maintain your stance.
- The nine necessities of defense are: transition; purpose; pressure on the ball; position—on the ball/off the ball; prevent penetration; move with every pass/dribble; ahead of the ball; blockout; and communicate.
- Defense on the ball includes defending the dribbler and live ball and dead ball situations.
- Defense away from the ball is the support phase of the defense. This helps the defender on the ball and protects the basket by guarding zone areas near the basket.

FIGURE 8-7 Fight through screens.

FIGURE 8-8 Switch screens—two-on-two hedge.

Assessment 8-1

Name   Section   Date

Description:

The basic four lines can be used with these added defensive options: *defensive zigzag; offensive and defensive zigzag*—in pairs without the ball (one offense, one defense going down the court—switch roles coming back); *offensive-defensive zigzag*—with the ball; *closeouts*—four offensive players at the free throw line extended. Four defensive players on the baseline with a ball pass to their partner and closeout to the ball.

Progression—no drive, drive right, drive left, pass to next person in line, and closeout again.

Rebounding—can set up similar to closeouts, but use one ball. All players should blockout in the power zone.

Assessment 8-2

Name _____ Section _____ Date _____

Description:

Three-on-three closeout—three offensive players at free throw line distance, rest of players on baseline. Teacher/coach starts drill by passing to any offensive player from under the basket.

Three-on-three, four-on-four halfcourt—can work on screens, rebounding, set plays, or special defensive rules; and can limit dribble or prevent all dribbling.

Three-on-three, four-on-four full court—teacher/coach can modify and provide progressions of choice; and no dribble or two dribbles or live.

CHAPTER 9

MOVEMENT WITHOUT THE BALL

OBJECTIVES

After reading this chapter, you should be able to:

- State basic principles of moving without the ball.
- Know and perform basic moves without the ball.
- Set and use offensive screens or picks.

KEY TERMS

While reading this chapter, you will become familiar with the following terms:

- ► Backdoor Cut
- ► Curl Cut
- ► Flare Cut
- ► Rear Cut
- ► V Cut

Performance Tip

Remove the magnet—you will be without the ball all of the time on defense and over 80 percent of the time on offense. Learn to move with a purpose when you aren't handling the ball.

One of the most difficult playing skills to learn is moving without the ball. This removes the magnet of the basketball and focuses on seeing the whole floor. You will play without the ball all of the time on defense and over 80 percent of the time on offense, so it is an important skill.

BASIC PRINCIPLES

Read the defense and the ball on offense—move to open spots on the floor to get open to receive a pass. Read and react to the defense. Get open yourself (to receive a pass) or get out of the way (screen for a teammate to allow them to get open, or keep your defender busy). Get open in the scoring position where you can shoot, pass, or drive.

Become an actor—act rather than react. Use believable fakes on offense when baiting the defender; act as a decoy. Learn to want the ball without begging for it. Be sure not to complain when you don't get the ball when you are open. Instead, keep moving.

Get lost from the defender—move out of the defender's field of vision. Most defenders have their backs to the basket with vision on the ball, so you should move behind defenders to the baseline and away from the ball before making moves back to the ball. Make the defender turn his/her head.

Run through leather when catching a pass—maintain your open position by meeting the pass, unless you are on a fast break/breakaway move to the basket ahead of the defender.

Get close to get open—an offense principle to free yourself from a defender. It is more effective to slowly get close to a defender and then make a quick cut to get open (action is quicker than reaction).

BASIC MOVES WITHOUT THE BALL

You will need to develop and use these moves to become a complete player in this area: stance, starts, steps, turns, stops, and jumps. These are the fundamental moves (Chapter 4) that need to be used with or without the ball, on offense or defense.

Special purpose cuts (moves) consist of: **V cuts** ("fake and break" moves), basic zigzag or change of direction cuts that form the path of a V. One side of the V is usually the move to the basket, away from the basket or to the defender (fake). The other side of the V is the quick change of direction cut to get open (break). Cuts to the ball are V cut moves to get open to catch a pass. Cuts to the basket are fast break moves ahead of the defense. **Backdoor cuts** are used when overplayed by a defender. To take advantage of a defender closing a passing lane, the backdoor cut can be used by two players. It requires precise timing and communication between teammates.

The player accomplishes this with ball faking the pass to the player without the ball to "bait" the defender. The player without the ball may also signal this move by coming to the "reverse direction" location and cutting back to the basket. Usually, getting open moves use a "hands up and ready" BP position. The footwork of the backdoor cut is usually a stride stop, a 180° reverse as shown on a rear turn and go move, as in Figure 9-1.

Front and **rear cuts** are moves after you have passed the ball to a teammate and want to challenge the defense by cutting to the basket for a possible return pass. This is one of the most valuable moves in basketball; it is sometimes called "give and go" or "pass and cut." The "give and go" takes two forms: the preferred front cut, which allows you to receive the ball in a passer-you-defender position (an excellent scoring position) and the rear cut, which permits you to cut behind the defender (to the basket) to gain an advantage going to the basket. A front cut uses a V cut to set up the defense while the rear cut is a more direct straight line cut.

When filling the lanes for the fast break, players without the ball should sprint (with their eyes on the ball) to assigned lanes up the court. They should beat defenders down the court by making an instant transition from defense to offense.

Transition moves from offense to defense require instant conversion to defensive assignments when ball possession is lost. Reaction moves require reading the teammate with the ball and reacting accordingly. When reading the defense the move should be made into the hole of the defense when slashing cuts are made.

FIGURE 9-1A The backdoor move—a stride step; the start of the "V" cut.

FIGURE 9-1B The backdoor cut to the basket—the end of the "V" cut.

As defenders change position on the floor, the players without the ball must read the defense and react to the new open areas.

Test the defense moves when offensive players are questioning the defenders motives. A player without the ball cuts through the defense (runs a through), the ball is reversed from one side of the floor to the other, or the defense is challenged by a cut or a dribble move.

Decoy moves, any of the basic moves, can be used to keep the defender busy (i.e., to distract a defensive player from helping defend a ballhandler or trap the ball). Learn to be an actor and a distracter.

" Shot" moves are to be used when the ball is in the air on a shot attempt by the offensive team. Each offensive player should either use a rebound move or go to a defensive assignment. You should never be a "ball watcher."

Mistake move—when you commit an error, you should "analyze and forget" it. You should focus attention on recovery, ask teammates for help by calling for help when needed, and hustle back to defense immediately. This is especially true when the error results in an interception.

Assigned moves refer to individually assigned cuts in a system of play for special situations. This includes jump balls, out-of-bounds, free throws, and set patterns. Players must carry out their assignment properly and quickly. How well it is done is as important as what is being done.

Setting and using screens are important. Getting a teammate open by setting a good pick or screen, and being able to use that screen are useful skills of individual offense.

SCREENS OR PICKS

Screens can be located on the ball (set on the ballhander's defender) or off the ball (set on a defender without the ball). Screens can also be set behind or out of a defender's vision (up screens) or set in front of or on the side of a defender (down screens). They also can contact a defender in front (front screen) or behind (rear screen).

Some coaches advocate screening a certain spot or areas on the floor (position screen) while some coaches believe in screening the defender (player screen).

▶ **V Cut**

An offensive move in the shape of a "V" used to receive the ball or get open.

▶ **Backdoor Cut**

A cut behind the defender and toward the basket against a defensive overplay.

▶ **Rear Cut**

An offensive move made as a player passes the ball to a teammate and makes a cut behind the defender to the basket for a possible return pass.

The latter is usually more effective in freeing the offensive player, but may result in more fouls caused by illegal screens (blocks).

To set a screen the screener should be as big and loud as possible in a legal BP. Use a noisy, jump stop with the feet shoulder width apart and the hands out of the screen (Figure 9-2). Your hands should be held over the groin area (men) or crossed over the chest (women) to protect yourself (Figure 9-3). Set a forceful screen so that the defender can see and hear it. Be loud, low, legal, and ready for contact. The screen should be perpendicular to the expected path of the defender; set it at the proper angle. Screeners should read and react to the defense and the cutter using the screen (usually opposite the cutter). This is shown by the common "pick and roll" play (Figure 9-4), the most frequently used on-the-ball screen. When the defenders attempt to fight through screens, the player using the screen is usually open. Thus, against switching defenses, the screener should set the screen and roll, or step out, the ball ready to receive the pass. Against good defensive teams, the cutter will usually be covered, but the screener will often be open. This means that the screener will most likely be open when a good screen is set and used. Screeners should set down screens against sagging defenders (back to the ball) or up screens against pressure or overplaying defenders (back to the basket).

FIGURE 9-2A Setting a front screen.

FIGURE 9-2B Setting a screen—using the front screen.

FIGURE 9-2C Setting a screen—illegal use of hands..

FIGURE 9-2D Setting a screen—a rear screen.

FIGURE 9-3A Protect yourself on a screen. Men should have their hands crossed over their groin.

FIGURE 9-3B Protect yourself on a screen. Women should cross their arms over their chest.

FIGURE 9-4A Screen on the ball—set and use the screen.

FIGURE 9-4B Pick and roll—roll when switch.

FIGURE 9-4C Pick and roll—hit "roll" player with bounce pass.

Prepare the defender to run into the screen (use a teammate as an obstacle) with a V cut, usually started toward the basket; cut razor close to the screener, shoulder to shoulder. Be in BP as you use and go past the screen with your hands up and ready to receive a pass. Wait for the screen to see and hear it, then move away from the ball screens. Read the defense and make the appropriate cut. When the defense sags **(flare cut)**; trails **(curl cut),** beats cutter over screen (backdoor cut), or gets screened (pop up behind the screen).

SUMMARY

- Offensive and defense moves without the basketball make up almost all of player's time during a game.
- The principles of offensive movement without the ball include: be ready to move; be aware of your teammates; move with a purpose; get open or get out of the way; be an actor; get lost (from the defender); run through leather unless on a breakaway; and get close to get open.
- The individual moves without the ball include: stance, starts, stops, steps, turns, and jumps. Special moves (cuts) include V cuts, to get open; cuts to the ball; cuts to the basket—fast break moves, backdoor cuts, front and rear cuts, and give and go moves.
- Filling the lanes on a fast break requires players to switch from offense to defense quickly.
- Reaction moves, decoy moves, assigned moves, and setting screens are basic moves without the ball.
- Screening rules should focus on the types of screens; position or player screens; setting low legal screens; and setting picks at right angles to the expected path of the defender. Then read and react to the defense by cutting or switching.

▶ **Flare Cut**
Offensive player breaking out behind a screen; used against a sagging defense.

▶ **Curl Cut**
An offensive move that breaks over the screen toward the basket and is used against a trailing defender or a cutting move in a half circle path around the screener.

Assessment 9-1

Name   Section   Date

Description:

The players should assume a basic four line drill position on the baseline. The player in each line moves from side to side without the ball, imagining it to be in the center of the court.

V cuts to get open (designated to the basket and to the ball or to the defender and to the ball); repeated V cuts followed by quick stops to simulate catching the ball the length of the court.

V cuts to get open followed by a backdoor cut. Proper foot work and hand position is emphasized (hands up—get open, outside hand down—backdoor).

Front cuts—a pass is simulated to the center of the court followed by a front cut (V cut—slow move away, fast cut to the ball) and quick stop at the free throw lines and the half line.

Rear cuts—a pass is simulated to the center of the court followed by a rear cut (change-of-pace, slow to fast) and quick stop at the free throw lines and the half line.

Note: Jump stops are used at each free throw line and half line. At the completion of each jump stop, the player should challenge the imaginary defense by using a "catch and face " move, in other words, quick stop, pivot and face the basket seeing the whole floor.

Progression:

One circuit each variation.

Learning Points:

Visualize - see the ball and the defender, then read and react to them; execute the skills properly and quickly; be quick in the right place and at the right time; jump stop under control - your hands should be ready to catch and chin the ball; "catch and face" the basket.

Assessment 9-2

Name	Section	Date

Description:

Three-on-three halfcourt games. All possible position and screening variations can be used: screens on the ball-pick and roll—guard, guard, forward—point, wing, wing—guard, forward, center; screens off the ball—curl, flare, backcut, and pop out.

Progression:

Walk through basic moves—defense stays, then switches; live offense, "no hands" defense; competitive—games to five baskets, make it, take it; designate starting position and allowed screens, with advanced players, allow all screening options; begin on the halfcourt, later incorporate into a three-on-three fullcourt team defense.

Learning Points:

Set and use screens; read the defense—cutter open, screener open, fake screen; use all screening rules—give feedback (what is right and what is wrong).

CHAPTER 10

CONCEPTS OF
TEAMWORK

OBJECTIVES

After reading this chapter, you should be able to:

- Understand general concepts of team play needed in basketball.
- Describe team offensive principles, positions, and components for basketball.
- Describe team defensive concepts, types, and levels for basketball.

KEY TERMS

While reading this chapter, you will become familiar with the following terms:

▶ Center

▶ Fast Break

▶ Guard

▶ Low Post

▶ Player-to-Player Defense

▶ Transition

▶ Zone Defense

Performance Tip

Highlight
Basketball is a unique team game that requires each player to play both offense and defense continuously. Your unique skills must be used to serve your team and produce the best team play.

Basketball is first and foremost a team game—you and a group of individuals uniting to form a team. It can be synergy, like the five fingers on a hand acting as one, so the hand can grasp or move together. The five players of a basketball team should display the same coordination. When it happens, that too, is special. The following are the essentials to prepare you for playing the team sport of basketball.

Teamwork means reaching your maximum individual and team potential. In basketball it is a supreme challenge to achieve. Your challenge is to develop your unique talents and serve your teammates.

The game of basketball is continuous. Positions don't mean a great deal as every player can end up playing at any position. All players must play offense and defense. Also, each player must perform the basic skills. Scoring is fairly easy; most players can create a scoring move alone. You don't need to work with your teammates; you just have a better chance for success when you do. This means that teamwork is in the hands of each player.

To develop the best team play possible you will need to: know your strengths and weaknesses (play within your limitations as you develop your talents); concentrate on giving your best; know and accept your team role; and work to improve your role in classes, practices, and the off-season. Find a way to make a positive contribution to your team.

OFFENSE

▶ **General**

One task for both teacher/coach and players is to plan, select, and develop a team offense that will allow a team to successfully meet every defensive situation. This includes: principles/player positions; fast break and press offense; set offense and formation (against player-to-player and zone defenses); and delay or control games; special situations, such as out-of-bounds, jump balls, free throws, and special plays.

▶ **Principles**

A basic offense should be used that can be adapted to a variety of players. It should be flexible enough to use the strengths of individual team members. Any offense should have court balance. In other words, produce high percentage shots with assigned offensive rebounders and assigned players for defense when a shot is taken. Balance also refers to proper court spacing—about 15–18 ft. apart—by offensive teammates. There should be ample opportunity for individual play (moves) within the team offensive framework. Balanced scoring from players is always better than the use of a "scoring star." A good offense includes player movement as well as ball movement. Scoring should be from inside (close to the basket) to outside (on the perimeter of the defense). This prevents the defense from concentrating on one area or one player. Execution of any system is more important than the system used. It isn't what you do, but how well you do it. Finally, there should be a smooth transition to defense after a made or missed shot. This is called the **transition** game, from offense to defense (and vice versa).

▶ Positions

Each player on a basketball team has a *position* to play. It is related to role, ability, and skill. The three basic positions in basketball are *guard, forward,* and *center* (or post). Some coaches use other names such as point, wing, and inside player.

The center is usually the tallest player with forwards next, and guards being the smallest. Centers and forwards tend to be the best rebounders while guards are often the best ballhandlers. Guards also tend to play "outside" more than forwards and centers.

Guards are usually called the team's *backcourt* when grouped together; separately named they are the *point guard* (usually the best ballhandler and often the player who directs the team on the floor) and the *shooting guard* ("big" guard or "off" guard). Point guards, because of their dribbling ability, are often able to create a scoring chance for a teammate (such as the shooting guard) by being able to *penetrate* and *pitch,* in other words drive to the basket past defenders and pass to an open or unguarded teammate. Directing teammates and creating scoring chances is the reason point guards are called *playmakers.*

Forwards are sometimes called *corner players* because their usual offensive position is in the corner of the frontcourt. There is usually a *small forward* and a *big forward* (sometimes called the power/forward or strong forward). The small forward is more of a "swing" player (guard or forward) and plays facing the basket where he/she must be a good ballhandler. The *power forward* is often a strong rebounder and "swings" from outside to inside (back to the basket).

The **center** is usually the biggest player and plays inside around the free throw lane, in the high post (near the foul line) or in the **low post** (close to the basket) and outside the free throw lane or three second lane with his/her back to the basket. The center and two forwards are collectively the *frontcourt.*

▶ Fast Break

One way for your team to get a good shot is the **fast break,** where the team that gains ball possession brings the ball upcourt before the opponents can get to a good defensive position. The fast break usually occurs after a rebound or steal and sometimes after a made basket.

As soon as ball possession is gained, the outlet pass or dribble (first move upcourt) is made to start the fast break. Then, you and your teammates attempt to beat the defenders upcourt while staying spread out. This is called *filling a lane* or coming in for a delayed shot, after performing a defensive safety role, to become a *trailer.* The fast break is the fastest way to make the transition from defense to offense. You should run at top speed under control when fast breaking. All players should pass first and dribble last when moving the ball up the court.

The ball should be taken to the middle of the court when the defense is outnumbered. The middle player should make a decision to pass or drive to the basket by the time the free throw line is reached. **NOTE:** The middle player goes to the free throw "elbow" after the pass for a possible return pass or ball reversal.

▶ Press Offense

If the defense is defending fullcourt (all over the court), you will need a *press offense* to get the ball inbounds safely. You should get the ball inbounds before the defense gets set. This is done by designating a frontcourt player to take the ball out after all made baskets and quickly inbounding the ball to a guard.

▶ Set Offenses

If the defense is set and waiting for you, a *set offense* should be used to get a good shot. It is recommended that your team have a starting formation then use the fundamental skill moves with and without the ball to create scoring opportunities. These moves are clearly described in earlier chapters where other offensive guidelines are discussed. The starting formations for a set offense may take a variety of beginning positions.

When a team has a lead late in the game or during a possession, it is sometimes sound tactics to spread out on the court and use the whole frontcourt to make the defense cover a larger area. This is called a *delay* game (or control game) and

---

▶ **Transition**
Changing from offense to defense and vice versa.

▶ **Guard**
A position at the top of the free throw lane (these players usually have excellent ballhandling skills).

▶ **Center**
Another term for the post position.

▶ **Low Post**
Area near the basket where inside offensive players usually operate.

▶ **Fast Break**
Getting the ball up the floor quickly for a score by outnumbering the defense.

usually only close to the basket or three-point field goal shots are taken. The most common formation for this offense is when four offensive players are placed in the four corners and the best dribbler is out front in the middle of the court. The playmaker constantly looks to "penetrate and pitch." All offensive players are watching for their defender to make an error to capitalize on. They "read and react" to the defender.

▶ Special Situations

Your team must have a plan when the ball is awarded to your team underneath your basket (under out-of-bounds) or on the sideline (side out-of-bounds).

Free throw situations need also be planned carefully to provide balance. On an offensive free throw (Figure 10-1), the two best rebounders should occupy the second lane spaces and attempt to gain an offensive rebound to the middle of the lane or to the baseline side. The defender at the top of the key is stationed in a position to be alert for any "long" rebound or loose ball that might be tipped out. This particular defender, O_1, has safety responsibilities on defense and must not let any opponent get behind him/her for a long pass reception or lay-up.

Defensive free throw coverage is shown in Figure 10-1. X_1 is the playmaker alert for a loose ball or long rebound. X_2 "blocks out" or checks the shooter by getting between the shooter and the basket. X_4 and X_5 check the opponents on their side of the lane (in the second lane space) while X_2 and X_3 rebound the middle area. When a defensive rebound is obtained all team members may make a transition to the fast break.

The smaller, quicker players defend your basket when the jump ball is at center circle. No matter what the formation, the ball should be tipped to an *open spot* (where two teammates are next to each other without an opponent in between).

No matter what the situation, formation, play, or system, remember that execution is the key. It is not what you do, but how well you do it.

DEFENSE

▶ General

The basic foundation of any team is its defense, the ability of a team to prevent the opponent from getting good shots. How solid is your team's defense? Can it carry you through any game, no matter what the circumstances? Team defense should be the very heart of your team strength because it is the most consistent phase of team play. You should found your team on this concrete, immovable, unchangeable element of the game.

"Genius is the understanding of things simple" could be applied to defense in the game of basketball. Defense and its value is a simple concept but its value is neither obvious, nor easy to understand. Offense is easy to see. Most offensive moves translate into points on the scoreboard. Most defensive moves do not lead

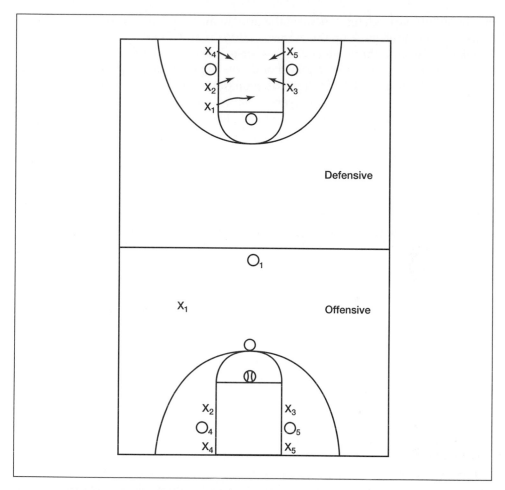

FIGURE 10-1 Offensive and defensive coverage for free throws.

directly to baskets. That's why it takes a greater understanding to look past the obvious relation of scoring to winning to the more important, though indirect, relationship of defense to winning.

Learn to play defense and build your team defense. With determination and practice you can become a good defensive player.

▶ Types of Defense

There are many varieties and styles of defense. Defense may be played at different levels of the court: *fullcourt*—defenders pick up or guard opponents as soon as possible all over the court (backcourt and frontcourt); *three-quarter court*—defenders allow the first inbounds pass and then pick up near the free throw line or top of the circle; *halfcourt*—defenders meet the opponents at the midcourt line; and *quarter court*—defenders pick up the offense at the top of the key.

Defense falls into three categories: **player-to-player**—each defender is assigned to a specific offensive player to guard or defend against; *zone*—you are assigned a floor area to be responsible for, depending on the position of the ball and the offensive players; *combination*—part player-to-player and part zone.

The player-to-player defense is the basic defense for all players to learn. The techniques can be applied in all defenses; therefore, it should be the primary, and probably the only defense used through the junior high school level of play. If you learn the basics of player-to-player defense, you will be able to adapt to any defense for high school, college, and adult recreation play. Pressure player-to-player defense is the most challenging and rewarding type of defense because it develops individual responsibility to the team. No defender can be hidden with this type of defense. The basic principles of this defense are explained in Chapter 9 on individual defense.

Zone defenses are designed to assign each defender to a certain area or zone, rather than to an opponent. Zones move as the ball moves and protect a limited area of the court. The weaknesses in a zone are in the "gaps" or "seams" (between defenders) and outside. Zones can also be varied to be *lane* defenses (try to intercept passes), *trapping* defenses (two players doubling up on one offensive player with the ball), or *sagging* defenses where the inside area near the basket is heavily protected.

The most common zone is the 2-3 zone. The 1-3-1 zone is also commonly used. It is strong in the center, wings, and point. The 1-3-1 zone shifts with the ball on the wing and in the corner. All zones revert to a 2-3 with the ball in the corner. The 1-2-2 zone has good coverage on the perimeter, but is vulnerable inside. The movement and shifts of the 1-2-2 zone are similar to the 1-3-1 zone.

Combination defenses usually take the form of triangle-and-two, two players use player-to-player action on selected opponents while three defenders play a triangular zone or box (diamond-and-one), one defender plays player-to-player while the other four play a box zone defense. This works well against a team with one outstanding scorer or ballhandler.

All team defenses are based on individual fundamental skills; take pride in your ability to play defense and make your team better.

SUMMARY

- Basketball requires you to develop your individual talents to blend in with your teammates to produce the best team.
- A team offense should be flexible, balanced (court, scoring, movement), executed properly, and designed to make a smooth transition to defense. You will play a guard, forward, or center position. The fast break is the first phase of team offense when you outnumber the opponents and beat them down the court to score an easy basket. When your team faces a pressure defense a press offense is needed to counter, penetrate the defense safely, and explore scoring

opportunities. Finally, you and your team will need to know what to do in the offensive special situations of free throws, out-of-bounds, and held balls.

* Defensively, you will need to use your individual defensive skills to fit into a team defense—player-to-player, zone, or combination. You will have to play defense at different levels and in all types of special situations.

▶ **Player-to-Player Defense**

A team defense where each defender is assigned a specific offensive player to guard.

▶ **Zone Defense**

A type of defense played when each player covers an area of the court.

CHAPTER 11

INDIVIDUAL
OUTSIDE MOVES

OBJECTIVES

After reading this chapter, you should be able to:

- Know and perform live ball moves.
- Execute dribble moves.
- Know and perform dead ball moves.

KEY TERMS

While reading this chapter, you will become familiar with the following terms:

- ► Crossover Drive
- ► Dead Ball Moves
- ► Direct Drive
- ► Jump Shot
- ► Live Ball Moves

Basketball is first and foremost a team sport. All players must learn to work together, but at the same time use individual offensive moves with the basketball. There is ample opportunity for use of your individual moves with the ball while four other teammates move without the ball. All five players, however, must closely coordinate these moves in a team situation.

Individual offensive moves with the basketball are divided into two categories. *Outside moves* are made past a defender when facing the basket. These moves are often made in scoring range on the perimeter of the defense. *Inside moves* are made past a defender with the back to the basket or facing away from the basket. These moves usually occur close to the basket near the free throw lane.

Individual outside moves consist of **live ball moves,** when the offensive player holding the ball still has a dribble available; *dribble moves,* when the offensive player is in the process of dribbling the ball (Chapter 5); **dead ball moves,** made at the completion of the dribble when a player has used the dribble and stopped in possession of the ball; and *completion shots,* shots taken on a dribble-drive move at the completion of the dribble.

LIVE BALL MOVES

Live ball moves begin from a BP with the ball in triple threat (TT) position (shoot, pass, or drive) facing the basket. The preferred technique of getting into TT position is to catch the ball in the air and land using a jump stop in a position facing the basket. When a player cannot land facing the basket in TT position, the alternative is to "catch and face." In other words, catch the ball with both hands, jump stop, and pivot in TT position to face the basket (Figure 11-1).

Performance Tip

Highlight

Outside, or perimeter, players need to establish a pivot foot and keep the ball in triple threat (TT) position. All players need to develop the basic live ball moves such as *direct drive* and *crossover drive.* The best *dead ball* or *completion move* to protect the ball is the "chinit" move.

▶ **Live Ball Moves**
When an offensive player has not dribbled.

▶ **Dead Ball Moves**
When the offensive player stops dribbling and picks up the ball.

Protect the ball. Keep it close to your body and use your body as a shield: triple threat; live ball move; chinit and pivot in defensive traffic; avoid dangling the ball, put it near your armpit.

Decide on a pivot foot philosophy. A permanent pivot foot (PPF) is when the nondominant leg is used as the pivot foot at all times. A right-handed player uses the left foot in pivoting while a left-handed player would use the right foot. This places the player in a shooting position with the dominant foot forward in a staggered stance. Either pivot foot (EPF) may be used as the pivot foot by both right- and left-handed players. The advantage of the EPF technique is its flexibility to meet all situations and its coordination with the jump stop (where either foot may be used as a pivot foot).

Conserve time and space. All moves should be quick and in a straight line toward the basket. Slight contact should be made with the defender as you dribble drive past. Use quick pass and shot fakes while maintaining BP. The live ball move (using the dribble drive past a defender) should be made with a quick first step with the lead foot past the defender toward the basket.

Attack the basket. You should accelerate under control on the dribble drive to the basket. Challenge the defense by being ready to pass to an open teammate. The objective of any live ball move in the power zone is to score a lay-up with one dribble (seldom are more than two dribbles needed).

Now or never. The live ball move is best made immediately after receiving a pass. Make the move before the defense can adjust and while the defense is moving. If in doubt, pass.

Attack the front foot. When the defender is in a staggered stance (Figure 11-2), his/her most vulnerable side is the front foot side. This is because a pivot and drop step must be executed before the defender can make an angle back move to cut off penetration. Therefore, it is helpful to be aware of the defender's front foot and use a live ball move to that side of the body when possible.

FIGURE 11-1 Catch and face (feet ready).

FIGURE 11-2 Attack front foot and then a direct drive move.

▶ PERMANENT PIVOT FOOT (PPF) MOVES

PPF moves should be used when a primary pivot foot is used for all live ball moves. The left foot should be used for right-handed players and vice versa.

The **direct drive** is the drive past the defender with the dominant foot. The right-handed player would drive past the defender's left side with the first step taken by the right foot (and vice versa). You need to establish TT position in a staggered stance; push off the pivot foot, explode with the free foot straight to the basket, push the ball to the floor and in front before the pivot foot is lifted, step past the defender with the PPF and attack the basket. The breakdown count consists of two actions: explosion step with dominant foot and push ball ahead to floor and dribble drive.

The **crossover drive** is a nondominant side move. It is the basic counter move to the opposite side when the defender overplays the dominant side. Establish TT position. Make a short "jab" step toward the defender, then cross the dominant foot over to the other side of the defender (and past) while keeping the ball close to your body when swinging it across at the same time, then push the ball ahead to the floor and dribble drive. Point your dominant foot at the basket. Your pivot foot is stationary while both the jab step and crossover drive are made with the *same* foot. The breakdown count consists of three actions: the jab step, swing your dominant foot and the ball over to the other side, and push the ball ahead to the floor and dribble drive. **NOTE:** The direct drive, hesitation drive, rocker step, and crossover drive are the basic four live ball moves needed to combat most defenders.

▶ EITHER PIVOT FOOT (EPF) MOVES

The following moves are to be used when EPF is used as the pivot foot for live ball moves. Both right- and left-handed players should be able to establish a pivot foot with either foot.

The EPF direct drive (direction foot) is used to dribble drive past a defender using the foot for the explosion step on the side being driven. Make a quick stop facing the basket. When driving right, use your left foot for a pivot foot and take an explosion step past the defender with your right foot (i.e., drive right, step with your right). Also when driving left, step with your left foot using your right foot as the pivot foot. Push the ball ahead on the floor and dribble drive. The breakdown count consists of one action: an explosion step with the lead foot on the same side as the dribble drive (right foot to right side, left foot to left side). (Figure 11-3).

The EPF direct drive (opposite foot) is used to drive past a defender on either side by using the opposite foot to step across and by shielding the ball as a direct

---

▶ **Direct Drive**
An offensive move in a straight line to the basket.

▶ **Crossover Drive**
The basic countermove to the opposite side when the defender overplays the dominant side.

FIGURE 11-3 EPF direct drive—direction of foot side.

FIGURE 11-4 EPF direct drive—opposite foot side.

drive is made. Make a jump stop facing the basket. When driving right, step past the defender with a left foot explosion step and push the ball ahead on the floor and dribble drive. The breakdown count consists of two actions: an explosion step past the defender by using your foot opposite the side of the dribble drive and push the ball ahead on the floor and dribble drive (Figure 11-4).

The EPF crossover is a countermove using either foot as the pivot foot (fake right, crossover left with your left pivot foot; fake left, crossover right with your right pivot foot). Make a jump stop facing the basket. Jab step and crossover with the same foot to the opposite side (swing the ball across and close to your body), then push the ball ahead on the floor and dribble drive. The breakdown count consists of three actions: jab step, crossover step with same foot while bringing the ball across, and push the ball ahead to the floor on the dribble drive (Figure 11-5).

DRIBBLE MOVES

The dribble moves used following all live ball moves are described in detail in Chapter 5, "Basics of Ballhandling." Proficiency in live ball moves should be coupled with the development of quick, controlled dribble moves.

▶ DEAD BALL MOVES

Dead ball moves are used at the completion of a dribble move when the quick stop is made close to the basket. They are best used within 10–12 ft. of the basket and can be used going to either the left or right. Protect the ball by using the "chinit" position, which may be needed if defensive pressure is faced. Keep the

FIGURE 11-5A EPF crossover drive—the start.

FIGURE 11-5B EPF crossover drive—step past the defender.

dribble alive whenever possible. The dead ball situation should be avoided unless a pass or shot is anticipated.

▶ EPF DEAD BALL MOVES

Take a **jump shot** by executing the quick stop and taking the jump shot with balance and control (see Chapter 6). Execute a shot fake and jump shot by doing a jump stop and a believable shot fake (lift the ball head high while maintaining BP with legs locked and taking the jump shot.

▶ COMPLETION SHOTS

All live ball moves and dribble moves will terminate in a pass, a dead ball move, or a completion shot. The completion shots most often used are the basic lay-ups described in Chapter 6, "Basics of Shooting."

SUMMARY

- Individual outside moves are the live ball, dribbling, dead ball, or completion moves.
- Live ball principles beginning in the basketball position (BP) facing the basket with the ball in triple threat (TT). Protecting the ball; decide on a pivot foot philosophy; use the straight line principle; attacking the basket; anticipate the defense; and, attack the front foot.

▶ **Jump Shot**
  Offensive shot attempted when leaving the ground with the feet.

- The dead ball move rules include: keep the dribble live whenever possible unless you have a shot; use dead ball moves after a jump stop close to the basket or a one-footed jump for a lay-up/jump shot; protect the ball by keeping the ball close to your chest, and use the "chinit" technique when necessary.
- The jump shot and shot fake and jump shot are EPF dead ball moves. Completion shots at the end of live ball situations include all types of basic lay-ups.

Assessment 11-1

Name   Section   Date

Description:

One-on-one, three-on-three halfcourt, and three-on-three fullcourt closeouts.

Progression:

One-on-one closeouts: There should be dummy defense play in position, but it should simulate a live defense. To help make the offense perfect, evaluate each move and give feedback. For example, allow the live ball move to the right or live ball move to the left by reading the defender. It is live defense games to five baskets. Make it, take it. You must score to keep the ball.

Three-on-three closeouts: Use individual outside moves in reaction to defenders as the opportunity presents itself.

Three-on-three halfcourt and fullcourt: Individual outside moves are used in reaction to defenders.

Learning Points:

Anticipate—see the ball; read and react to the defense, avoid forcing a move; pass first, dribble last; use outside moves only when appropriate within the team concept; and, be quick at the right time and catch and face every time the ball is handled; use the quick stop and the pivot; and attack the basket.

Assessment 11-2

Name   Section   Date

Description:

Begin on the baseline of the fullcourt. Carry out a live ball move, dribble move, and a dead ball or completion move toward the other basket. Simulate beating a defender on each move. Repeat coming back up the court. Develop either a PPF or an EPF technique. The following variations should be used: direct drive, speed dribble, lay-up; crossover drive, crossover dribble moves, lay-up; direct drive, dribble move, jump shot; crossover drive, change-of-pace move (alternate speed and control dribble), jump shot; choice of PPF (or EPF "choice" move), spin dribble moves, jump shot; choice of live ball move, choice of behind-the-back or between-the-legs or back dribble moves, dead ball moves.

Learning Points:

Anticipate—see the ball; read and react to the defense, avoid forcing a move; pass first, dribble last; use outside moves only when appropriate within the team concept; and, be quick at the right time.

Assessment 11-3

Spin Pass Outside Moves

Name   Section   Date

Description:

Using the halfcourt area, spend concentrated practice time on live ball moves and completion or dead ball moves from a simulated pass catching situation. Use the two-hand underhand spin pass to yourself in all primary offense locations and situations: spin pass to yourself in spot locations near the edge of the three-point field goal line. Or catch the ball on the first bounce with your feet in the air and land facing the basket. Or catch and face every time the ball is handled. Use the jump stop and the pivot. Attack the basket. Periodically use a playing partner or teacher/coach to evaluate your technique. Only excellent practice makes excellent technique. Spin pass to yourself in primary locations on the halfcourt. Catch the ball in the air; land facing away from the basket; and pivot and face the basket in TT position. Use either PPF or EPF technique for developing footwork. Practice appropriate live ball, dribble and dead ball, or completion moves using all the basic principles. A tossback training device may be used in conjunction with the spin pass technique to simulate passing/catching situations to be used with the outside moves.

Learning Points:

Develop a variety of game moves from primary locations and situations. Pass accurately to yourself. Catch and face the basket in all situations. Challenge the imaginary defender and see the whole floor. Maintain eye contact on the basket whenever possible. Use peripheral vision to see details on the rest of the court. Visualize the defender by reading and predicting his or her moves. Make game moves at game speed. Follow every shot until it is in the basket (i.e., rebound each shot). Use a playing partner for periodic evaluations. Use shot and pass fakes when practicing all moves. You should develop these fakes as a natural part of your game.

CHAPTER 12

INSIDE MOVES
FOR POST PLAYERS

OBJECTIVES

After reading this chapter, you should be able to:

- State reasons for a strong inside game.
- Understand principles for inside players.
- Execute post shots and power shots.
- Understand and perform facing moves.

KEY TERMS

While reading this chapter, you will become familiar with the following terms:

- ► Facing Moves
- ► Post Line
- ► Post Shot
- ► Power Move

Most coaches and players recognize the importance of establishing an inside game with a post player receiving a pass near or inside the free throw lane area.

The inside game can produce a high percentage shot because of the scoring opportunities when available so close to the basket. When a post player takes the ball to the hoop among numerous defenders and he/she is fouled when shooting, this is a three-point play. The defense collapses allowing a three-point field goal scoring opportunity. The post player passes the ball outside again. It reduces pressure defense on the perimeter. When outside defenders help on an effective inside post player, it is difficult to establish and maintain outside defensive pressure. It is a skill that requires a minimum of ballhandling and can be learned with practice. Post play is the chance to build the offense from the inside out. Inside moves are considered back to the basket scoring moves, usually from a low or medium post position.

BASIC PRINCIPLES

Get the ball inside. The ball must penetrate the perimeter of the defense on a regular basis (by the dribble drive or the pass to a post player). Use the backboard on most inside moves when shooting; especially on a 45° angle, when using a power move, or in an offensive rebound situation.

Assume inside players are stationed close to the basket therefore they can be primary rebounders. The shooter best knows the exact location and timing of the shot. Thus, a post player using an inside move should always assume the shot will be missed and prepare to rebound from BP with the elbows out and hands ready (head high).

All players are post players, and some of the best inside players have been medium- and large-sized people. Technique is more important than size. A more critical factor is relative size; you should be able to "post up" a defender of similar size or smaller.

Inside players need to create contact and use their bodies to control the defender. The inside area is frequently congested, so the offensive player will often face physical contact situations. Be in balance with BP.

Keep both hands up inside. Passing to inside players is difficult and challenging and there is little margin for error due to congestion and limited time constraints (in the lane). Thus, inside players should always be prepared to receive a quick pass from a teammate.

Performance Tip

Highlight

Establish an inside-out attack for more consistent offense.

Use crisp air passes. Most passes to post players are quick, accurate air passes delivered the instant the post player is open. For smaller post players the bounce pass may be used.

POSITION

Get in a post player stance. The inside or post player must develop the ability to assume an exaggerated BP. They must use a wider base, have a low center of gravity, keep the elbows out and parallel to the floor as extensions of the shoulders, and hold the hands up and slightly forward with fingers spread and pointing to the ceiling (Figure 12-1).

Provide a two-hand target. The hands should be up and ready. Post up on the **post line.** The inside player should attempt to get open just outside the free throw lane, near the free throw line "block" and close to the post line. Getting a position on the post line shortens the pass from the post feeder. Ideally, the post player would be posted up with shoulders square (at right angles) to the post line.

Get open by using a basic move without the ball such as the offensive zigzag (i.e., V cut). Make contact, then rear turn to "seal" the defender from the passing lane; flash cut to the openings between defenders. Get behind the defenders and out of their vision and cut to the openings and toward the ball to post up (Figure 12-2).

Create contact and stay open. The defender has taken a defensive position, make contact and keep the defender in place. Keep your feet active, be big, use the whole body and create contact with defender on your hip. You should also use antennas (rear bumpers) to maintain contact.

CATCHING THE BALL INSIDE

Read the pass. The passer "feeding" the post player should pass to the hand target away from the closest defender. The location of the pass will tell the post player the location of the defender when the pass is thrown.

Keep the passing lane open. The feet are active and contact is maintained until the ball is near the receiver. Face the ball.

Catch the ball with two hands, with your feet in the air, and with a slight jump stop (except when fronted). Catch the ball with your eyes.

Chin the ball for possession and protection.

Lob or reverse when the defender establishes a ball-defender-post player position. With the lob-over-the-top (Figure 12-3), the passer shows the ball and uses a check pass

FIGURE 12-1 Post player stance.

FIGURE 12-2A Get open in the post position—"V" cut to get open.

FIGURE 12-2B Get open in the post position—"V" cut end.

(pull the string) to read the "help-side" defensive coverage. The pass is thrown quickly over the defender to the junction of the backboard and rim. The post player faces the base-line and establishes contact with the defender on his hips and buttocks with both hands up and in BP (palms facing passer). The post player waits until the ball is overhead before

FIGURE 12-3 Lob pass to the post.

releasing to catch the ball with two hands. The ball is reversed to high post or helpside. If a defender is fronting on one side of the floor, the ball may be reversed, as the defender is "sealed off" and the post player steps to the ball.

Take the defender out of the play. If you are defended on the low side, then start lower. If you are defended on the high side, then start higher. If you are fronted, start closer to the ball. And if you are being played behind, step into the lane before posting up with a V cut or rear turn.

READING THE DEFENSE

When the defender is fronting the post player the outside player feeder should use a lob pass over the defender or reverse the ball, pin the defender, and feed the

► **Post Line**
The straight line through the ball and the basket.

post from the opposite side. A power move or reverse lay-up should be used on the lob play. When the defender is behind the post player, this player will catch the ball and face the defender. If the defender is on either the low side (baseline side) or the high side then the post player can use the power move.

Read and react by contacting. Read the pass, turn toward the middle, find an opening in the defense, and make a move to the hoop or pass off to an open teammate.

INSIDE MOVES

The **post shot** is the basic tool for the post player; therefore it is an essential scoring weapon. This shot was illustrated and explained in Chapter 6. The move is usually made without the dribble.

The **power move** is used to the baseline side when the defender is on the high side (away from the baseline). This move may also be used toward the middle when the defender is on the baseline side. After the post player catches and chins the ball by using a rear turn pivot on the foot closest to the defender, seal off the defensive player with your "bumpers"; take one power dribble (both hands/hard bounce) between your legs as you do a hop from both feet and execute a jump stop, landing facing the baseline (belly baseline). This dribble can sometimes be eliminated when close to the basket. Use a power move to score with your shooting hand away from the defense. Protect the ball with your body and use the backboard when possible. See Figure 12-4.

FIGURE 12-4A Power move—catch, chinit, and score.

FIGURE 12-4B Power move—a two-hand dribble and hop.

FIGURE 12-4C Power move—two-foot stop and chinit.

FIGURE 12-4D Power move—use the power shot.

Facing moves are used when the defender is playing behind the post player, especially with a defensive gap. The offensive player pivots with a front turn (on the baseline foot) or with a rear turn on either foot. Use a jump shot or a shot fake (lift) with a jump shot (see Figure 12-5). Live ball moves may also be used; rear turn on either pivot foot—jump shot, jump shot with lift and live ball moves. This move tends to clear the defender and create a gap for the quick jump shot.

▶ **Post Shot**

A back to the basket shot by an inside offensive player, similar to a hook shot or lay-up from the chinit position.

▶ **Power Move**

An offensive shot close to the basket while in traffic, usually shot off the backboard after a jump stop.

▶ **Facing Moves**

Used when a defender is playing behind the post player, especially when there is a defensive gap.

FIGURE 12-5 Post player—catch and face the hoop.

SUMMARY

• The post player's position can create for the team great scoring opportunities such as the "three-point play." An effective post player needs to make contact, have his/her hands up ready for the pass, and read the defense. After catching the ball a post player has many shooting moves to choose from including the post shot move, power move, and the facing moves.

Assessment 12-1

Name   Section   Date

Description:

The basic drill to teach the fundamentals of post play. The teacher/coach is the feeder (passer) for players posting up in designated ways. The variations are: to designate a move to get open (use both sides of key area); post or power moves; and facing moves—jump shot or fake and jump shot.

Learning Points:

Do it right then do it quickly; perform game moves at game speed; give a target, read the pass, chin the ball and read the defender; challenge the defense; be alert for open teammates. The teacher/coach places an assistant at selected locations. The post player must pass to the assistant whenever he/she is open. Put hands up in the ready position. Be strong and make contact to locate and control the defender. Be ready for contact on the move. Assume the shot will be missed and get the ball back to the teacher/coach with a quick, accurate outlet pass.

Assessment 12-2

Name   Section   Date

Description:

Two offensive and two defensive players work on post play from various locations around the free throw lane. All offensive and defensive post play principles are applied. When defenders obtain possession the first outlet pass or dribble may be made.

Progression:

The two-on-two post play drill may be first used in games to five baskets, then progressed to make it, take it with the score being kept during a given period.

Assessment 12-3

Name   Section   Date

Description:

A post player uses a spin pass (or pass and rebound from a tossback) on the desired post location with his/her back to the basket. Three repetitions of each post move are made on each side of the free throw lane. The inside move sequence consists of post to middle; power to baseline to middle; face jump shot, fake and jump shot, or live ball move (rear turn option).

Progression:

Skeleton post moves. Call move, read the pass; move against dummy defense, designate defender's position; dummy defense, the defender varies defensive position (read and react); live defense.

Learning Points:

Meet the pass, chin the ball; visualize the defender; make quick moves with good technique; assume the shot will be missed, keep rebounding until the shot is made; practice at top speed, but under control and do not pause between repetitions, the action should be continuous.

CHAPTER 13

CONDITIONING—
MENTALLY AND PHYSICALLY

OBJECTIVES

After reading this chapter, you should be able to:

- State reasons for conditioning.
- Identify basic conditioning areas.
- State basic strength guidelines.
- State basic stretching rules.
- Perform basic stretches.
- Understand nutritional guidelines.

KEY TERMS

While reading this chapter, you will become familiar with the following terms:

- ► **Balance**
- ► **Conditioning**
- ► **Nutrition**

- ► **Stamina**
- ► **Strength**
- ► **Stretching**

The "winner's edge" should be your approach to conditioning. Several guidelines are most important to obtain that edge:

- **Balance** your approach to living and conditioning. Moderation and balance are the keys to success.
- What you do off the court is as important as what you do on the court. This includes eating, drinking, sleeping, and physical activities. Treat your body with respect.
- Mental and physical conditioning are essential to success.
- Maintain a high level of conditioning year round. Build fitness and living habits for life. Conditioning is a changing quality that must be maintained and developed as long as you live.
- One measure of condition is called body composition. It is an indicator of the amount of fat stored in the body. Excess fat limits performance and endangers health; the recommended range is 10–20 percent for men and 15–25 percent for women, with an optimal range of 5–15 percent for men and 10–20 percent for women. This can be found by measuring skinfold or by a water submersion test. A body fat measure is a much better indicator of your fitness than weight. Your teacher/coach can usually measure your body fat with skin calipers.
- Warm up and warm down should always be done. Treat your body with respect. Move moderately before and after you play.

Conditioning depends on the development of sound practices in four areas: *strength*—the ability of your muscles to contract and control your movement; *stretching*—the mobility and flexibility of your muscles, tendons, and joints; *stamina*—the endurance of your body, both muscle stamina and the stamina of your heart and lungs; and *nutrition*—the nutrients that you take into your body will determine how close you come to your potential.

STRENGTH

Strength development is needed to improve your potential to move—run, jump, stop, start, and play the game. The stronger your muscles, the better you can perform as a basketball player. There are several principles of strength development.

▶ **Balance**
The primary principle of body movement; body control.

▶ **Conditioning**
A changing quality that must be maintained and developed in life.

▶ **Strength**
The development of muscles that can improve your potential to move—run, jump, stop, start, and play the game.

- Specific strength building programs using weights and machines are seldom necessary before junior high school. Avoid excessive heavy strength programs when the body is going through heavy growth and development, especially with the bone structure of the body.
- Strength programs should be supervised and tailor-made. They should be balanced and should cover the major muscle groups. The American College of Sports Medicine recommends doing one set of 8–12 repetitions for 2–3 times per week with each major muscle group.
- Be sure to observe all safety procedures to protect your body and build strength without injury. Develop a balance of strength in opposing muscle groups. Certain strength ratios must be developed and maintained. Get expert advice and supervision. You should also balance strength and stretching. Exercise through a full range of motion and combine strength building with stretching. Do your strength programs on a year-round basis.

STRETCHING

Stretching of tendons, muscles, and other tissues is beneficial to basketball players. Flexibility programs can help you prevent injuries, move easier, and perform better.

Warm up the body before doing stretching exercises. Running slowly is a good method of warming up. Stretch before and after you practice and play. Perform each movement slowly and forcefully, eliminate any bouncing or jerking. Perform slow easy stretches and continue to the point of a slight pain or burning sensation, hold that position for 10–15 seconds, or 3–5 deep breaths, then recover and relax the muscle. It is also helpful to contract or tighten the muscle then relax and stretch it for best results.

Performance Tip

Individual Stretches

Ankle rolls (out, in)	Lower back twister
Ankle plant or flexor	Lower back cat curl and stretch
Quad stretch	Lower back hyperextend (arch)
Calf stretch/wall stretch	Shoulder stretch
Hamstring stretch	Finger and wrist stretch
Groin stretch/seated cross	

STAMINA

Stamina or endurance is the most important area of fitness for a basketball player. Basketball is a true test of stamina for every player because it is a game of continuous movement. If you want to find the most likely area to gain the "winner's edge" in conditioning, it is the area of endurance.

There are many ways to measure your level of stamina, from your informal feelings as you play the game to formal measures of endurance. The simplest test is Kenneth H. Cooper's twelve minute test *(The New Aerobics)*. In Cooper's test, you run as far as you can in twelve minutes and compare your performance to the following table:

Distance (miles)	Endurance
Over 1¾	Excellent
1½ to 1¾	Good
1¼ to 1½	Average
1 to 1¼	Poor
Less than 1	Very Poor

Another measure of stamina is resting heart rate or pulse rate. As you get in better condition, your resting pulse rate tends to go down. You can take your own pulse on the wrist or to the left or right of your Adam's apple.

You need to overload the heart and lungs to improve endurance to develop stamina for basketball. Your heart rate taken right after exercise (pulse rate) is the best measure of overload. You need to reach a certain target pulse rate to develop stamina. This depends on your age. In general, a heart rate of 150–160 beats a minute must be reached and maintained for a minimum of 20–30 minutes at least three times per week.

One of the best ways to overload the body to develop stamina is to duplicate the motions of basketball and practice the game. Conditioning is specific to the activity. It is best if endurance is developed while basketball skills are developed; work hard as you practice and play.

Interval training is the recommended approach for basketball stamina building. This consists of short, intense periods of activity with intermittent periods of rest. This type of program simulates a basketball game, with short, intense bursts of

▶ **Stretching**
Stretching increases flexibility, which can prevent injuries and helps you move better.

▶ **Stamina**
Endurance is the most important area of fitness for a basketball player because the game requires continuous motion.

activity and short rest breaks during free throws and jump balls. Sprinting for short distances, 100 yards, 200 meters, or courts widths and lengths. The rest period should be three times as long as the time spent exercising or running. For example, twenty second sprints would be followed by a sixty second rest period (continue moving or walking) and repeated 6–10 times per workout. The heart rate can be checked immediately after each sprint during the rest period. Strenuous stamina conditioning should be preceded by a warm up such as jogging and stretching and followed by a similar warm down.

NUTRITION

Attention should also be given to **nutrition,** a critical part of your conditioning program. The three elements that will contribute most to your physical condition are: *specific conditioning programs,* strength/stretch/stamina; *adequate rest,* it will affect your play the next day; and *a well-balanced diet,* treat your body with respect. Remember, "garbage in, garbage out."

Your body is like a machine and food is fuel. If you eat the right food, your body works smoothly and efficiently. If not, it won't get the nutrients it needs and won't perform as well.

Common sense tells us that we must eat right to play at our best. It doesn't take a genius to learn to eat right. It isn't necessary for you to get special food at a health store, take special vitamin supplements, or add extra protein to your diet. You do need to know some basic facts to get the necessary vitamins, minerals, carbohydrates, fats, proteins, and water your body needs.

There is no scientific proof that a large intake of vitamins or protein improves basketball performance. Select a variety of foods from the food groups (see list) and you will provide your body with the essentials.

Proteins, fats, and carbohydrates are the energy sources for the body. Carbohydrates are the body's most usable energy source and should be about 60 percent of your diet. The best source of "carbos" is whole grain breads, fruits, and vegetables.

We strongly recommend simple nutrition guidelines. Your diet should be low in fat (less than 20 percent) and high in fiber (complex carbohydrates). The test is your stool—if your feces floats, you are eating right; low in sugar and salt and balanced (variety); high in water, the most important nutrient. Drink before and beyond thirst.

Refined foods should be eliminated or reduced. Candy, cakes, butter, margarine, and other snack food provide energy only, and when not used right away become fat.

It is critical to follow the Food Guide Pyramid and get plenty of water as an essential part of your diet. Drink water when you are thirsty and even when you are not. The rule is "drink before and beyond thirst." A lack of water can cause fatigue, lack of mental alertness, dehydration, and overheating of the body.

Eat and drink right. Treat your body with respect.

MILK GROUP - select two servings daily

Foods	Nutrients	Minerals	Vitamins
Nonfat Milk	Protein	Phosphorus	A, C, D
Nonfat Cottage Cheese		Calcium	Niacin
Nonfat Yogurt			Riboflavin
Ice Milk			Thiamin
Lowfat Cheese			

MEAT GROUP - select two servings daily

Foods	Nutrients	Minerals	Vitamins
Beans-Lentils	Protein	Iron	A, C, D
Beef-Liver	Fats		Niacin
Eggs-Nuts			Riboflavin
Fish-Pork			Thiamin
Heart-Veal			
Kidney			

FRUITS and VEGETABLES GROUP - select at least five servings daily

Foods	Nutrients	Minerals	Vitamins
Green and Yellow	Carbohydrates	Calcium	A, C
Fruits and Vegetables		Iron	Riboflavin
		Magnesium	

BREAD and CEREAL GROUP - select at least six servings daily

Foods	Nutrients	Minerals	Vitamins
Enriched, Whole Grain	Carbohydrates	Calcium	A, C
Breads/Cereals	Some Protein	Iron	Riboflavin
		Magnesium	

▶ **Nutrition**

Diet is the crucial part of a conditioning program. The food is fuel for the body. Remember, "garbage in, garbage out."

SUMMARY

- Conditioning for basketball requires development of sound practices in four areas: strength, stretching, stamina, and nutrition. Each is important in the development of a healthy body and mind.
- Strength programs should be set up by a professional trainer to insure safety and proper techniques.
- Stretching can be a daily activity whether it is before and after you play basketball or working on increasing your flexibility. Stretching can help prevent injuries.
- Basketball is a game of constant motion. Endurance is developed as you work and play hard on the basketball court.
- Pay attention to your nutrition when exercising. A well-balanced diet fuels your body.

APPENDIX A:

Checklists—Basketball Skills and Self-Appraisal

FREE THROW CHECKLIST

Alignment	Vertical plane. Front foot turned in and pointed to backboard edge.
Grip	Shooting hand—form V, spread fingers, cock and lock wrist, index finger on airhole.
Elbow	Up and in and under ball.
Weight	Forward at start and end.
Target	Back of rim (FOCUS).

GENERAL PRINCIPLES

SEE AND SAY NET.

Technique	Pause at the bottom of shot, then shoot smoothly, positive motion toward the basket.
Release and follow through	Shoot up and over, be firm but relaxed, put hand in basket and hold follow through until net.
Feedback	Make—praise self; Miss—analyze and correct.
Ritual	Do It The Same Every Time.

SHOOTING CHECKLIST

GENERAL PRINCIPLES

Balance	Start from floor, feet ready, body ready, head straight.
Grip	Shooting hand—fingers spread; Guide hand—side or under.
Wrist	Cock and lock.
Elbow	Up and in and under ball.

Target	Board—upper corner of rectangle; Rim—back of rim to see the eyelet.
Up and over	Thrust fingers, snap wrist through the ball, backspin.
Follow through	Controlled relaxation; make a parachute and hold it one count.
Concentrate	Focus and visualize; get your rhythm.

FIELD GOAL PROGRESSION

Form shots	To self- wall- backboard, check grip—backspin follow through.
Killer shots	Start in close and work out.
Shots from a pass	Underhand spin pass to self, wall, tossback or with partners.
Shots from dribble	Go somewhere to left and right.
Competition	Percentage, consecutive number, with others.
Feedback	Make—praise; Miss—analyze.

REBOUND CHECKLIST

OFFENSIVE BOARDS

Assume	every shot will be missed.
Anticipate	see ball, know areas; be aware of ball, rim, and players.
Be a garbage rebounders	want the ball, find a way.
Know objectives	make contact; get to a gap; pressure rebounder.
Hands up	body position (BP), with elbows shoulders high.
Develop scoring moves	tips, overheads, power, fakes.
Chinit	when in traffic.

DEFENSIVE BOARDS

Assume	every shot will be missed.
Know best areas	helpside, middle, ballside.
Develop skills	see ball; assume; pressure shot; see player; go to player; blockout; go to ball; capture ball; chin ball; outlet ball (go-bump-go/capture-keep ball).

Self-Appraisal Checklist
Individual Skills Checklist

Evaluation Scale:
Legend: Excellent—(E); Good—(G); Satisfactory—(S); Needs Work—(NW)

Skill	Player's Name	(E)	(G)	(S)	(NW)	Comments
Stance						
Starts						
Stops						
Turns						
Jumps						
Individual Defense —Off Ball						
Individual Defense —On Ball						
Individual Defense —Off to On (closeouts)						
Individual Defense —Post						

Skill	Player's Name	(E)	(G)	(S)	(NW)	Comments
Individual Defense —General						
Offensive Rebounding						
Defensive Rebounding						
Dribbling						
Pass—Catch						
FG—Shooting						
—Layup						
—Set/Jump Shot						
—3 Pt. Shot						
FT Shooting						
Individual Moves —without ball						
Individual Moves —with ball outside perimeter play						

Skill	Player's Name	(E)	(G)	(S)	(NW)	Comments
Individual Moves —with ball inside post play						
Team Play						
Transition D to O						
Transition O to D						
General						

COMMENTS:

163

GLOSSARY

ANGLE JUMP: Diagonal jumping move toward the basket by a defender moving to the ball while rebounding.

ASSIST: A pass from an offensive player to a teammate resulting in a basket.

BACKBOARD: A flat rectangular surface rebound device placed behind the basket in a vertical position.

BACKCOURT: The area of the court from the halfcourt division line to the defensive endline.

BACKDOOR: A cut behind the defender and toward the basket against a defensive overplay.

BALANCE: A primary principle of body movement; body control.

BALL SCREEN: An offensive player comes to a teammate with the ball to screen the defender on the ball.

BALLSIDE: A position one pass away from the ball that is within passing range and unobstructed by another player; also the side of the court on which the ball is located.

BALLSIDE OR FRONT CUT: A move by an offensive player toward the basket and to the ball in front of the defender.

BALL-YOU-BASKET: The desired relationship of a defender guarding the player with the ball and the basket (a straight line relation).

BALL-YOU-PLAYER: The desired relative position for a defender guarding a player without the ball (in relation to a player with the ball).

BANK SHOT: A shot, usually taken from a 45° angle with the backboard, which bounces against the backboard and falls into the basket.

BASEBALL PASS: One-hand pass to advance the ball up the court, similar to an overhand baseball throw.

BASELINE: The court boundary line underneath either basket on both ends of the floor.

BASKET: The ring, goal, or rim; it is usually 18 inches in diameter and is attached to the backboard.

BASKETBALL POSITION (BP): The ready position for movement skills.

BLOCK-AND-TUCK: A technique used to catch the ball thrown to the side of the body to stop the pass with one hand (block) and bring it into the body with both hands (tuck).

BLOCKING: Illegal personal contact that impedes the progress of an opponent.

BLOCK OUT: A rebounding position with the rebounder making contact and staying between the basket and the opponent.

BLUFF: A defender faking at a ballhandler to impede his/her progress.

BOX: The area on the free throw lane near the basket that is shaped like a square or box and used as the lower free throw lane space marker.

BOUNCE PASS: A pass between offensive players that hits the floor in between the pass and the catch.

CATCH AND FACE: Catch the ball, square up and face the basket and see the whole court.

CENTER: Another term for the post position.

CENTER OF GRAVITY: The imaginary weight center of the body.

CHANGE OF PACE: When a player alternately slows down and speeds up his/her pace.

CHARGE: A push by a player against an opponent in a legal position (a foul).

CHEST PASS: A two-handed pass thrown from chest level.

CHINIT: A ball protection position of the ball directly under the chin with the elbows and fingers up and the body in BP.

CLEAR: When an offensive player vacates an area so another offensive player with the ball can maneuver.

CLOSED STANCE: Denial position of the defender with hand in the passing lane, ball-you-player being guarded. The thumb of the hand is down, with palm facing the ball.

CLOSEOUT: Advancement of a defensive player toward an offensive player with the ball.

CONTROL DRIBBLE: Low dribble used against defensive pressure.

COVER DOWN: The defending players collapse into the lane to help defend against ball penetration and movement of offensive players to the line of the ball.

CROSSOVER DRIBBLE: Dribble from one hand to the opposite hand across and in front of the body.

CROSSOVER DRIVE: An offensive live ball move; jab step fake followed by an opposite side step before dribbling past defender.

CURL: An offensive move that breaks over the screen toward the basket and is used against a trailing defender or a cutting move in a half circle path.

CUT: An offensive move, usually toward the ball, basket, or a teammate.

DEAD BALL: When the offensive player with the ball stops dribbling and picks up the ball.

DEFENSE: The team trying to keep the opposing team with the ball from scoring.

DEFENSIVE BLUFF: A body fake used by a defender to keep the offensive player with the ball off balance.

DENY PENETRATING PASS: A defensive tactic to prevent the offensive pass to the middle of the floor inside the halfcourt defense and near the free throw lane.

DIRECT DRIVE: An offensive move dribbling with the ball in a straight line to the basket.

DOUBLE DRIBBLE: A violation that involves dribbling again after stopping a dribble or dribbling with two hands at the same time.

DOUBLE TEAM (TRAP): A defensive ploy with two players guarding one offensive player.

DRIBBLE DRIVE: A dribble move toward the basket.

DRIBBLER: Offensive player moving the ball on the court by legally bouncing it with one hand.

EITHER PIVOT FOOT (EPF): An offensive technique in which either foot is used to pivot.

EXPLOSION STEP: A long, quick step used by an offensive technique in which either foot is used to move past the defender.

FAST BREAK: Getting the ball up the floor quickly for a score by outnumbering the defense.

FIELD GOAL: A successful basket attempt that counts two points or three points (not a free throw).

FIELD GOAL PERCENTAGE: The rate of the field goals made to field goals attempted.

FLARE: Offensive player breaking outside behind a screen; used against a sagging defense.

FLAT TRIANGLE: A defensive position held between the offensive player with the ball and the offensive player being guarded (the pistols position); one step off the line of the ball and player you are guarding.

FORECOURT: The offensive area of the court from the top of the key area to the endline (baseline).

FREE THROW: A free shot given to a player as a result of an opponent's foul (counts one point).

FREE THROW PERCENTAGE: The rate of free throws made to free throws attempted.

FRONTCOURT: The offensive area of the court from the half line to the endline or baseline.

FRONT TURN: A pivot in which the front of the body moves forward.

FUNDAMENTALS: Basic skills involved in playing the game of basketball.

GAP: The distance between the offensive player and the defensive player.

GO TO THE FIRE AND FIGHT OUT: A defensive transition to the danger area near the goal and then out to find an offensive player to defend.

GUARD: A position at the top of the free throw lane (these players usually have excellent ballhandling skills).

GUARDED: When an offensive player is being checked or defended by a defensive player.

HALF LINE: The line in the middle of the court separating the frontcourt and backcourt.

HELP AND DECIDE: Defensive term used when a defensive player assists a teammate with an offensive player and returns to the offensive player being guarded or switches assignments.

HIGH POST: Offensive position in the area of the free throw line.

JUMP SHOT: Offensive shot attempted when leaving the ground with the feet.

JUMP STOP: Common name for the "one count" quick stop, landing with both feet at once.

JUMP TO THE BALL: Defensive position by moving to the ball while keeping a flat triangle.

KEY: Another term for the free throw lane that originated with the first lanes, shaped more like a key with a narrow lane and a wide circle.

LAY-UP: Close shot made when moving to the basket.

LIVE BALL: Term used when an offensive player has not dribbled.

LOW POST: Area near the basket where inside offensive players usually operate.

MIDCOURT: Area of the frontcourt between the half line and top of the key.

OFFENSE: The team trying to score by legally putting the ball through the basket.

OFF THE BALL SCREEN: Offensive screen away from the ballhandler.

OPEN STANCE: Defensive position almost parallel to the ball while watching your opponent and the ball; used in flat triangle position two passes away from the ball (also called a "pistols" stance).

OUTLET PASS: Pass made to an offensive player up the court by the rebounder, usually to start a fast break.

OUT-OF-BOUNDS: Area outside the boundary lines of the playing area.

OVERHEAD PASS: Pass made while having the ball above the head with both arms extended.

PALMS FACING: A player with his/her hands in a vertical position facing forward.

PALMS UP: A player with his/her hands in a horizontal position facing up.

PARALLEL STANCE: Heel-to-heel relationship of feet (from front to back).

PASSING LANE: Area between two offensive players where a pass could be made.

PENETRATION: When an offensive player dribbles inside the defense toward the basket or a pass moves toward the basket.

PERMANENT PIVOT FOOT (PPF): An offensive technique in which all pivots are made from the nondominant foot.

PICK: Screen by an offensive player.

PIVOT: Rotation of the body around one foot that is kept in a stationary position.

PLAYER-TO-PLAYER DEFENSE: A team defense where each defender is assigned a specific offensive player to guard.

"POINT YOUR PISTOLS": Defensive position that involves pointing one hand at the offensive player being guarded and the other hand at the offensive player with the ball. Also called an open stance.

POST: A position in or immediately outside the free throw lane line, and the player positions with his/her back toward the basket.

POST SHOT: A "back to the basket" shot by an inside offensive player, similar to a hook shot or lay-up from the chinit position.

POWER LAYIN: An offensive shot close to the basket while in traffic, usually made off the backboard after a two-foot stop.

PUSH PASS: A one-hand pass from a triple threat position made with a bent elbow start.

QUICK JUMP: A jumping motion from a hands up, knees bent position that happens fast.

READY POSITION: Stance with the knees bent, the hands up and ready, and with the head up and looking forward.

REAR CUT: An offensive move made as a player passes the ball to a teammate and makes a cut behind the defender to the basket for a possible return pass.

REAR TURN: A pivot in which the "rear" rotates backward.

REBOUND: Catching the ball off the backboard or rim after a missed field goal or free throw attempt.

RECOVERY: Gaining the ball after a turnover.

RETREAT STEP: A defensive backward step after an offensive player advances, used to maintain a defensive gap.

REVERSE: A 180° change of direction, or changing the ball from one side of the court to the other.

RITUAL: A familiar routine that a player shooting a free throw should use on every shot.

SCREEN: Legal action by a player who, without causing contact, delays or prevents an opponent from reaching a desired position.

SECOND SHOTS: Offensive shots taken after gaining an offensive rebound.

SHOOTING POCKET: Triple threat offensive ball position.

SHOOTING RANGE: Distance from the basket in which an offensive player can make a designated percentage of shots.

SPACING: A balanced team offensive positioning where offensive players are 15–18 ft. apart.

SPEED DRIBBLE: A high, quick dribble up the court by an offensive player.

SPIN DRIBBLE: An offensive pivoting move that occurs while dribbling and changing direction; sometimes called a whirl dribble.

SPLIT VISION: The ability to see the court using peripheral vision.

STAGGERED STANCE: Basketball position or stance with one foot in front of the other foot in a heel-to-toe relationship.

STRIDE STOP: "The two-count" stop where one foot touches the floor before the other.

STUTTER STEPS: Short, choppy steps taken in a controlled motion.

SWITCH: A defensive tactic of changing the offensive players being guarded on defense.

TEAM PLAYER: A player willing to sacrifice individual recognition for team success.

TRANSITION: Changing from offense to defense and vice versa.

TRAP: A double team of two defensive players on one offensive player with the ball.

TRAVELING: When an offensive player with the ball illegally advances the ball by running or walking; a violation.

TRIPLE THREAT: An offensive position where a ballhandler is facing the basket with the ball in a position near the dominant shoulder such that the player can quickly pass, shoot, or drive. The position is called "pitting the ball."

TURNOVER: An error that causes the offensive team to lose possession of the ball.

V CUT: An offensive move in the shape of a "V" used to receive the ball or get open.

VIOLATIONS: Infractions of the rules that result in loss of the ball.

WEAKSIDE: A position that is more than one pass away from the ball because of distance or another player obstructing the direct passing lane; also the side of the lane opposite the ball.

WING: A perimeter position on the side of the basket outside the free throw line.

WRIST BACK LAY-UP: An offensive shot close to the basket and off the backboard with the hand behind the ball.

ZONE: A type of defense played when each player covers an area of the court.

SUGGESTED READINGS

Barber, B. 1996. *A basket for Allie*. New York: Lee & Low Books.

Blais, M. 1995. *In these girls, hope is a muscle*. New York: Atlantic Monthly Press.

Brittenham, G. 1995. *Complete conditioning for basketball*. Champaign, IL: Human Kinetics.

Davenport, J. and M. Adrian, eds. 1992. *Basketball monographs: Ideas for today's game*. Reston, VA: American Alliance for Health, Physical Education, Recreation and Dance.

Douchant, M. 1995. *Encyclopedia of college basketball*. Detroit, MI: Visible Ink Press.

Frey, D. 1994. *The last shot: City streets, basketball dreams*. Boston, MA: Houghton Mifflin Co.

Harkins, H. and J. Krause. 1997. *Motion game offenses for men's and women's basketball*. Champaign, IL: Sagamore Publishing Co.

Harkins, H. and J. Krause. 1997. *Zone offenses for men's and women's basketball*. Champaign, IL: Sagamore Publishing Co.

Harkins, H. and J. Krause. 1997. *All purpose offenses for men's and women's basketball*. Champaign, IL: Sagamore Publishing Co.

Harkins, H. and J. Krause. 1997. *Three-point field goal offenses for men's and women's basketball*. Champaign, IL: Sagamore Publishing Co.

Hult, J. S. and M. Trekell, eds. 1991. *A century of women's basketball: From frailty to final four*. Reston, VA: National Association for Girls and Women in Sport.

Jensen, J. 1996. *Beginning basketball*. Minneapolis, MN: Lerner Publications.

Joseph, P. 1996. *Basketball*. Minneapolis, MN: Abdo & Daughters.

Krause, J. 1991. *Basketball skills and drills*. Champaign, IL: Human Kinetics.

Krause, J. 1994. *Coaching basketball*, Indianapolis, IN: Masters Press.

Lieberman-Cline, N. 1996. *Basketball for women: Becoming a complete player*. Champaign, IL: Human Kinetics.

Lobo, R. 1996. *The home team: Of mothers and daughters, and American champions*. New York: Kodansha America.

Miller, D. 1995. *The carr creek legacy*. New York: Vantage Press.

Nelson, G. 1992. *Elevating the game: Black men and basketball*. New York: Harper Collins.

Robinson, A. 1996. *David Robinson*. Grand Rapids, MI: Zondervan Publishing House.

Stewart, M. 1996. *Isiah Thomas*. New York: Children's Press.

Walker, C. 1995. *Long time coming: A Black athlete's coming-of-age in America*. New York: Grove Press.

INDEX

Note: Page numbers in *italics* indicate illustrations.